HAPPINESS, DEATH, AND THE REMAINDER OF LIFE

The Tanner Lectures on Human Values

JONATHAN LEAR

HAPPINESS, DEATH, AND THE REMAINDER OF LIFE

HARVARD UNIVERSITY PRESS

Cambridge, Massachusetts

London, England   2000

First Harvard University Press paperback edition, 2001

Permission to quote from Franz Kafka's "The Great Wall of China," in the Everyman's Library edition of the *Collected Stories* (1993), granted by Alfred A. Knopf, Inc., a division of Random House, Inc.

Library of Congress Cataloging-in-Publication Data

Lear, Jonathan.

Happiness, death, and the remainder of life / Jonathan Lear.

p. cm. — (The Tanner lectures on human values)

Includes bibliographical references (p.) and index.

ISBN 0-674-00329-2 (cloth)

ISBN 0-674-00674-7 (pbk.)

1. Psychoanalysis and philosophy. 2. Ethics. 3. Freud, Sigmund, 1856–1939.

4. Aristotle. I. Title. II. Tanner lectures on human values (Cambridge, Mass.)

BF175.4.P45 L42 2000

150.19'5—dc21   00-039705

FOR BERNARD AND PATRICIA WILLIAMS

CONTENTS

Human nature, essentially changeable, unstable as the dust, can endure no restraint; if it binds itself it soon begins to tear madly at its bonds, until it rends everything asunder, the wall, the bonds, and its very self.

—**FRANZ KAFKA**, "The Great Wall of China"

HAPPINESS

What difference does psychoanalysis make to our understanding of human existence? I want to focus here on a particular aspect of civilized existence: our life with values. What difference does psychoanalysis make to our understanding of ethical life?

Psychoanalysis teaches us that wish, if not hope, springs eternal. Here is a wishful thought which comes quickly to mind when we begin to think about psychoanalysis and ethics. Might it not be possible to expand our understanding of ethical life to take account of the fact that human beings live with unconscious motivations? The idea would be to use psychoanalysis to devise a more humane ethics—one which considered humans more fully and realistically before saying how they should live. The prospect might then open for some kind of reconciliation of individual human desire with the needs of society and civilization.

The tradition I am concerned with grounds ethical life in the development and expression of character. Perhaps the greatest achievement in this tradition lies at its origin—in Aristotle's ethics. For Aristotle, character is a developmental and psychological achievement. We are habituated into certain character formations by our parents, family, and teachers, who get us to act in certain ways repeatedly, before we can understand the reasons for doing so. We thereby develop certain stable psychic dispositions—to see and think about the social environment in certain ways and to act accordingly. This is our "second nature." Now, for Aristotle, certain character-formations are better than others. Those that facilitate the living of a full, rich, meaningful life—a *happy* life—are the human excellences, or virtues.

The attraction of this character-based approach is that it purports to account for ethical life in terms of the lived realities of human motivation and judgment. Consider, for example, human kindness.[1] This character trait is not on Aristotle's own list of the virtues, but we do not have to stick to that list to preserve the overall ethical spirit. A kind person will have a distinctive sensitivity to the world—and a special sort of motivation to act. To be truly kind, one needs to be able to distinguish a situation in which one ought to step *in* and help someone who is struggling, from a superficially similar situation in which one should step *back* and allow the struggling person to develop the requisite skills and sense of autonomy. A kind person will be sensitive to that difference—and in noticing that difference will thereby be motivated to act in the appropriate ways. On this character-based approach, there is no way to specify, in a particular set of circumstances, what is the kind thing to do independently of the judgment of a kind person.

I shall discuss the structure of the virtues in the next lecture, but already the hope of an expanded Aristotelianism is coming into view. After all, if ethical life is an expression of character, and character itself can be shaped by the psychologically enlightened training of parents and teachers, why can we not include our understanding of the unconscious in that training? We might then differ with Aristotle over what the best character formations are—a happy life might come to take a different shape from the one he imagined—but the overall approach would be Aristotelian in spirit.

It is a thesis of these lectures that such a project cannot work— and, in coming to see why not, we shall learn about the psychoanalytic unconscious and about the attempt to ground ethical life in character. In brief, I want to argue that the unconscious is too disruptive to be contained in any straightforward account of character formation.

Ironically, this project of including the unconscious in ethical character formation would be unassailable if psychoanalysis were one more science among others. On this normalized understanding, psychoanalysis would be distinctive because of its hitherto unexplored subject matter, the unconscious. In opening up a new realm of inquiry, psychoanalysis would be adding to our knowledge. On this conception, psychoanalysis is an extension of what philosophers tend to call "folk psychology." Folk psychology is the attempt to explain human action on the basis of beliefs, desires, and intentions to act. Indeed, its first systematic exposition is in Aristotle's ethics. Of course, the term "folk psychology" is somewhat unfortunate insofar as it suggests that these are the mental states people ordinarily ascribe to one another before they are in the grip of some particular psychological theory. In fact the situation is almost the reverse. People regularly ascribe all sorts of complicated motivations and emotional states—including unconscious ones—to one another. And they talk about "folk psychology" only after they are in the grip of a philosophical theory about the elementary explanation of action. Nevertheless, one can see the idea that is at play: folk psychology would have to be expanded to include unconscious wishes and fantasies along with beliefs and desires, but then we could formulate a character-based ethics designed to take account of the whole kit and kaboodle.

But psychoanalysis is not another science in any normal sense: about this, the critics are right. Indeed, it seems not just mistaken but ultimately complacent to treat it as such. For what psychoanalysis uncovers is not a new area of knowledge so much as something disturbing about ourselves. Could there be a non-disturbing way of doing this? By now it is, perhaps, a too-familiar idea that in life we somehow keep the unconscious at a distance. The process which Freud called "making the unconscious conscious" could not, he thought, be a straightforward discovery, but necessarily involved transformation of the soul. It always involved uncovering something disturbing—and the uncovering always occurred under conditions of resistance and repression. Should the uncovering be so fraught in ordinary life, but theorizing about it be straightforward? Or might the apparent straightforwardness of psychoanalytic theory itself be part of the covering over?[2]

But if in theory and in practice the unconscious is always being covered over, it is also always already present and manifest in the coverings over. It is this intuition I want to take back to the first systematic attempt to work out a psychologically minded ethics. The question then becomes, not "What do we have to *add* to Aristotle?" but rather "What is already there in Aristotle's ethics, disturbing the self-presentation, yet not quite conscious of itself?"

This question is of more than historical interest. For we live at a time when the promising approaches to ethics are broadly Aristotelian in spirit. Philosophical culture has grown weary of rule-based approaches to ethics. By now, the critiques of Kant's attempt to ground morality on the moral law are well known.[3] In briefest outline, from the moral law it is impossible to derive any specific conclusions about how to act in a specific set of circumstances. It is, in part, because this critique has become widely shared that there is a renewed interest in Aristotle. For Aristotle, it is precisely because it is impossible to specify a set of rules on how to act well that one must turn to a psychologically informed account of how to build good character.

Interestingly, this is an approach that Freud himself ignored. Freud's critique of ethical value is itself addressed to a certain law-based interpretation of the Judeo-Christian tradition. This interpretation focuses on the Ten Commandments, the Mosaic Law, the injunction "Love thy neighbor as thyself," and so on. As I shall discuss in the third lecture, Freud was concerned with a certain inexorability of unconscious guilt which life within this ethical tradition tended to facilitate. Being brought up in the Law tended to produce in individuals cruel superegos, set up over against the ego, judging it harshly and inflicting ever-greater punishments and inhibitions. This was Freud's diagnosis of life within civilization. But Freud more or less equated life within the Law and life within the ethical, and he thereby overlooked this alternative, Aristotelian approach.[4] For Aristotle seems to hold out the prospect of an ethics based on an integrated psyche in which values are harmoniously expressed in a genuinely happy life. Is this, then, a real possibility that Freud simply ignored? It is striking that Freud turned to ancient Greece for its myths, but not for its ethics or philosophy. Returning to Aristotle thus opens up the possibility of a different type of psychoanalytical reflection on the ethical.

Of course, psychoanalysis is itself concerned with the returns we feel inclined to make. And there seems little doubt that in contemporary philosophical culture the *Nicomachean Ethics,* whatever else it might represent for us, has become a fantasy of origins. It is where we return when we want to work our way back to the origins of an alternative to law-based approaches to ethics. And psychoanalysis teaches us to suspect that if there is a disturbance within the ethical, we ought to find at least hints of it at the origin. Certainly, the disturbance ought to be gaining some expression in the fantasy of origin. So this ought to be a return with a difference. The hope is to find out more, not just about Aristotle, but about ourselves in our previous goings-back. What have we had to overlook in order to treat Aristotle as an origin? What doesn't get seen in order to preserve the fantasy? In answering those questions, we may start to gain insight into the distinctive difference psychoanalysis makes.[5]

There is, I believe, reason to question the foundations of the Greek ethical experience. One can glimpse the problem at the first moment in which Aristotle invites us to participate in ethical reflection. For the very first sentence of the *Nicomachean Ethics* induces a reflective breakdown. "Every art and every inquiry, and similarly every action and choice, is thought to aim at some good; and for this reason *the* good has rightly been declared to be that at which all things aim."[6]

As generations of commentators have noted, the inference is invalid. From the fact that every art, inquiry, action or choice aims at some good, it simply does not follow that there is one good at which all things aim. There has been no shortage of articles criticizing Aristotle—here the oedipal struggle and the desire to get tenure converge—but are we really to think that the founder of formal logic committed such a flagrant fallacy? More insightful commentators assume that Aristotle could not be making such a blunder, and so there have also been ingenious attempts to make this sentence come out right. According to one of the best attempts to make sense of this sentence, Aristotle is here trying to state what the supreme good *would be* (if there were such).[7] The problem for this interpretation is that there is no textual indication that Aristotle is speaking hypothetically; indeed, he seems to emphasize that the good has *"rightly been declared"* (καλῶς ἀπεφήναντο) to be that at which all things aim. I suppose one can add "if there were such a thing," but it seems an interpretive stretch.

This looks like a dilemma: Either one accepts that Aristotle made a logical error in the opening sentence of his fundamental ethical work or one must make coherent sense of what he is saying. Rather than choose, however, I should like to shift the question away from what Aristotle is saying and ask instead what he is doing. I would like to suggest that Aristotle is here participating in a peculiar kind of *inaugural instantiation*. He is attempting to inject the concept of "the good" into our lives—and he thereby changes our lives by changing our life with concepts.

Aristotle does not do this on his own. For an inauguration to be successful there must be a context in which it occurs. The relevant context in this case is the Greek philosophical effort—notably of Socrates and Plato—to found ethics as a form of practical-rational inquiry. For Socrates, the fundamental question is "How shall one live?" Ostensibly Socrates is asking a question, but ultimately it makes more sense to see him as attempting to introduce a concept—the concept of "a life"—into life. We are now challenged to consider *our lives* in deciding what to do.

Why think of this as the introduction of a concept rather than, say, an invitation to reflect upon a concept we already possessed? One of the twentieth century's most significant contributions to philosophy—manifest in the work of the later Wittgenstein and of Heidegger—is a working through of the idea that there can be no viable distinction between the existence of concepts and the lives we live with them. There can be no fundamental divide between thought and life. If we consider the confusion, anxiety, and anger that Socrates generated, there is little doubt that the Athenian citizens had, in Socrates' time, no way to think about the question he was asking. Indeed, Socrates regularly confused himself. One has only to read the *Charmides* to see Socrates get himself into serious confusions as he tries to think about how to think about one's life. And in the *Apology* Socrates famously says that he discovered the oracle that he was the wisest of men was right because of his peculiar ignorance. Although he did not know, at least he knew that he did not know, and that alone made him wiser than anyone else. But if no one knows the answers to the questions Socrates is asking—if, indeed, no one really knows how to go about finding an answer—then there is reason to believe that Socrates is not asking well-defined questions but is rather trying to introduce new ways of thinking and living. This is the context, as elaborated by Plato, in which Aristotle injects "*the* good" into our lives.

Aristotle takes himself to be merely extending the locus of our preexisting concern with our lives. But remember the case in Wittgenstein of a person who takes himself to be going on in the same way with the instruction "Add 2," but who at some point in the series starts going on in what we take to be strange ways: 1004, 1008, 1012 . . .[8] We realize in his bizarre goings-on that he hasn't really grasped the concept—or that he is operating with a different concept which we do not yet understand. Now look what happens *to us* when Aristotle invites us in the first sentence to move from a concern for the various goods in our lives to a concern with *the* good: we are stumped; we need his lectures to teach us how to go on. From a Wittgensteinian perspective, this is evidence that, whatever he says he is doing, Aristotle is inducting us into a new way of life.

Jacques Lacan and the later Wittgenstein have, each in his own way, argued that a successful inauguration will tend to obscure its own occurrence. Lacan takes as an example the introduction of the concept of irrational numbers.[9] Once we have the concept of irrational numbers, it will look as though they were always there, awaiting discovery. But if we take the later Wittgenstein and Heidegger seriously, this cannot be right. Life before the "discovery" of irrational numbers was not "missing" anything. People lived with lengths, with numbers. The decision to apply numbers to lengths changed our lives with numbers and lengths: it opened our lives to new possibilities, to new ways of living and thinking. For the later Wittgenstein it only looks as though the irrational numbers were already there, waiting to be discovered, because our lives with numbers have fundamentally changed. Retrospectively, it will look as though earlier life without the concept of the irrational was incomplete, missing something. But that is because we are now embedded in a life with the concept, and it has become difficult to see any earlier form of life as anything other than incomplete.

Now if we go back to the first sentence of the *Ethics,* we can see an attempt to cover over its inaugurating nature. Aristotle himself says almost nothing about goods or the good: his assertion is basically about what others have thought and said. "Every art . . . *is thought* to aim at some good": strictly, Aristotle is passing on some high-class gossip. Rhetorically, the claim presents itself as a certain kind of received knowledge—common knowledge of the right sort of group. Indeed, part of what it is to be in this group is to take it as obvious that this is what "is thought." Notice the impersonality and passivity: "and for this reason the good has . . . been declared . . ." No one in particular is doing the declaring: impersonally, it is thus. No doubt, Aristotle's audience would have thought of Plato—it is hardly a secret who has done the declaring—but the sentence construction pushes one away from the activity of Plato's activity and steers one in the direction of accepting something as common knowledge. In particular, the sentence tends to keep from explicit awareness that Plato's own declaring might itself have been part of this inaugural instantiating activity. Aristotle enters explicitly in his own voice only with the word "rightly": "the good has *rightly* been declared." His own activity here is all but effaced. Notice too that the inference is constructed in such a way as to suggest that there is no real question whether there is any such thing as *the* good—it is presented as though it has always already been there—the only question is what it might be like. In these ways the performative activity embedded in this first sentence is hidden from view.

If the performance had succeeded, the sentence would have looked obviously true to us. Conversely, inaugural attempts will tend to draw attention to themselves when they misfire. Instead of looking as though it has always already been there, waiting to be discovered, in a failed inaugural attempt something will look odd, as though it doesn't fit in. This is what is happening in Aristotle's first sentence: Aristotle does not quite succeed in inaugurating "*the* good." Perhaps it is a fact about us that we can no longer take this sentence as obvious; and if it is not obvious, it must inevitably provoke some discomfort. It is worth getting clear about what is disturbing us.

In effect, Aristotle is trying to introduce the concept by means of which it would make sense for humans to take a teleologically oriented interest in their lives. For him, the birth of ethics as a serious reflective inquiry simply is the introduction of the concept of *the* good as the concept in terms of which one should reflectively evaluate one's life. Aristotle insists that this is of immense practical importance: "Will not the knowledge of it, then, have a great influence on life? Should we not, like archers who have a mark to aim at, be more likely to hit upon what we should. If so, we must try, in outline at least, to determine what it is."[10] It should now be clear that for Aristotle's act to succeed the audience must remain unaware of its inaugurating nature. For Aristotle is, in effect, injecting the teleological into life, and that act cannot itself be understood in teleological terms. It is too strong to say that this insight is repressed. Nevertheless, to grasp the inaugurating aspect of this act is to burst open the form of knowing and living that it attempts to create.

One can now see how Aristotle could make his way effortlessly to the end of his first sentence—and expect his intended audience to follow along. In the context of a teleological worldview, it makes sense to inquire about *the* good for us. It is *we* who cannot follow along who are in the less comfortable position of realizing that we can no longer live like that. We can no longer live like that, in part, because we are no longer living like that: thus our discomfort with the very first sentence. And thus our mild disquiet about what else might be opened up in that recognition. For once we become alive to the idea that Aristotle might be engaged in an inaugural act which, by its very nature, would tend to cover itself, the overall argument begins to look more suspicious.

Consider, for example, how Aristotle justifies his claim. He points out that the goods we already recognize often form hierarchies.[11] The design and making of a bridle, for example, are ultimately evaluated by the contribution it makes to military victory. The suggestion seems to be that we could keep on going. But once we become suspicious, it becomes evident that there are significant asymmetries. First, in the familiar hierarchies, we already know what the master good is. In this case, it is military victory. Second, in these cases the master good already functions in determining the shape of the lesser goods. So, to continue the example, the goal of military victory does filter down and influence the shape of the bridles that are made. That is, the familiar hierarchies tend to work *from the top down:* the overarching and known good influences the shape of the lesser goods. Now Aristotle has suggested that, in considering these familiar hierarchies, we could just keep going in order to form the conception of a larger, all-encompassing hierarchy. But this is moving *from the bottom up*— and Aristotle has given us no clue how to do this. It would seem we have been invited to move in the wrong direction.

Aristotle goes on to argue that if there were not this final goal, desire would be vain: "If, then, there is some end of the things we do, which we desire for its own sake (everything else being desired for the sake of this), and if we do not choose everything for the sake of something else (for at that rate the process would go on to infinity, so that our desire would be empty and vain), clearly this must be the good and the chief good."[12]

It is surprising that this argument has not caused more anxiety among readers. There is, of course, a reason for a fairly complacent reading: We know that the intended audience for these lectures is people who are well brought up and mature.[13] And we assume the lectures are intended to produce some form of intellectual and practical comfort: "to those who desire and act in accordance with a rational principle knowledge about such matters will be of great benefit."[14] That is why we tend to read the second conditional— "and if we do not choose everything for the sake of something else (for at that rate the process would go on to infinity, so that our desire would be empty and vain)"—as offering a *reductio ad absurdum*. But suppose we don't assume from the start that the absurd is impossible. That is, suppose through a certain form of reflection we become aware that desire is inherently slippery. Then this line of reasoning would open up the real possibility that our desire *is* empty and vain. That is, this reasoning would open us to anxiety.

Of course, the first of Freud's two major discoveries is that unconscious desire is inherently slippery. (I shall discuss the second discovery in the next lecture.) But even ordinary reflection gives us grounds for suspicion. We know that desire must settle to some extent for us to be able to act, but we also know that it is possible, indeed usual, for us to act on the basis of limited reflection. In general, a person can tell us to some extent what he is doing and why. But, if called up short for a full accounting, it is typical for a person's account of his own desires to trail off, perhaps pointing vaguely in some direction.

Aristotle's argument seems designed to intrigue his readers. He invites us to reflect on the absurdity of the idea that desire does not have an end, yet he also insists that it is mysterious what that end might be. Mysterious, yet of the greatest practical importance: "Will not the knowledge of it have a great influence on life?" Indeed, it seems that Aristotle is tempting us when he invokes the image of the archers. The implication seems to be that his inquiry will provide us with that distant mark which up until now we have lacked. If so, it would seem that Aristotle wants to have it both ways. He wants to keep us at a safe, perhaps complacent, distance from anxiety; but he also wants to suggest that without this knowledge we are missing something of the greatest importance for our lives.

Suppose Aristotle had brought us precisely to this point of the argument—and then just left us here. Wouldn't he have brought us into a position that he just declared absurd? That is, we would be desiring everything for the sake of something else (a something else which we could not yet specify because it purportedly lay just at the horizon of our understanding, but we hadn't yet been given the mark).

Imagine a courageous person who had not yet engaged in much ethical reflection—that is, an ideal member of Aristotle's audience. Such a person, when asked why he did something, would say, "because it was the right thing to do." He may, of course, be able to say more about what bravery is, what are the pleasures and dangers involved, but he wouldn't be trying to justify or explain his bravery by referring to some desire outside of his bravery. In other words, he would be lacking that distant mark which Aristotle's ethical reflection purports to be about to introduce. But then it would seem that the effect of introducing this distant, important, but as-yet-unknown mark is to open the virtuous person to the possibility of anxiety. For he is now being invited to understand his action in terms of *the* good—the archer's mark which has thus far only been mentioned, not yet shown. Of course, being virtuous, he will not *feel* anxious: anxiety is not a possibility he will take up. But to see that the impact of the argument is to introduce anxiety as a possibility, imagine Woody Allen getting this far in the argument, and then, left by his teacher to his own devices: "Wait a minute, you're telling me there's some distant mark in terms of which all my actions will or will not make sense—and now you want to leave?!" On the surface it looks as though Aristotle is about to provide us, the virtuous, with some ultimate reassurance for the lives we are already living. But if he is about to give us that, the fact that we don't yet have it must mean that, at the moment, we are lacking something important.

Aristotle thinks he can turn to politics to give us a glimpse of the archer's mark. To complete the passage begun above:

> Will not the knowledge of it, then, have a great influence on life? Shall we not, like archers who have a mark to aim at, be more likely to hit upon what we should? If so, we must try, in outline at least, to determine what it is and which of the sciences or capacity it is the object. It would seem to belong to the most authoritative art and that which is most truly the master art. And politics appears to be of this nature; for it is this that ordains which of the sciences should be studied in a state, and which each class of citizens should learn and up to what point they should learn them; and we see even the most highly esteemed capacities to fall under this; e.g., strategy, economics, rhetoric; now politics uses the rest of the sciences, and since

again, it legislates as to what we are to do and what we are to abstain from, for the end of this science must include those of the others, so that this end must be the good of man. For even if the end is the same for a single man and for a state, that of the state seems at all events something greater and more complete both to attain and to preserve; for though it is worth while to attain the end merely for one man, it is finer and more godlike to attain it for a nation or for city-states. These, then, are the ends at which our inquiry, being concerned with politics, aims.[15]

This passage is more problematic than it appears. First, this is the only case in which Aristotle tries to cite the end via the art, science, or capacity that is directed toward it. In every other case, it is the other way around. Architecture, for example, is the craft directed toward building houses, buildings, monuments. In politics, by contrast, we do not know what the good is ahead of time. Rather, Aristotle points to the inclusiveness of politics to suggest that *the* good, whatever it is, must be in its purview. Is this reversal a symptom?

Second, Aristotle is trying to reassure us that we have some actual grounds that there really is such a good. After all, we do have politicians legislating; the polis is the arena in which meaningful human activity occurs, and legislation does help shape that activity.[16] But if we look to actual activity, politics gives us little grounds for hope, and strong grounds for pessimism. Isn't Aristotle writing in the wake of the Peloponnesian War? In the aftermath of Socrates' death? It seems hardly likely that Aristotle was unaware of Plato's claim, put in Socrates' mouth in the *Gorgias,* that if the good is the end of politics then Socrates is the only true politician.[17] But if that is so, the claim "We'll know what the good looks like when we watch the activities of real politicians" turns into "We'll know what the good looks like when Socrates runs the state." We might as well wait for pigs to fly. The seeming appeal to the actual to justify the claim loses its force.

Third, the question of the political is deferred. I do not believe that any previous scholar has noticed that, if translated properly, the last line of the *Nicomachean Ethics* is identical with the last line of *Portnoy's Complaint:* "So [said the doctor]. Now vee may perhaps to begin. Yes?"[18] Here is the revised Oxford translation: "Now our predecessors have left the subject of legislation to us unexamined; it is perhaps best, therefore, that we should ourselves study it, and in general study the question of the constitution, in order to complete to the best of our ability the philosophy of human nature . . . Let us make a beginning of our discussion."[19] In other words, in the closing lines of the *Nicomachean Ethics,* Aristotle admits that any serious political study of the good has gone unexamined by his predecessors and it is only now time for him to begin. But at the beginning of the *Ethics* it was precisely political activity that was supposed to reassure us that there was a supreme good at which one might aim.

Even in the opening paragraphs of the *Ethics,* Aristotle seems implicitly to recognize that it is hard to tie his subject matter down. "Let us resume our inquiry and state . . ."; "Let us, however, resume our discussion from the point at which we digressed"; "Let us again return to the good we are seeking, and ask what it can be";

"but we must try to state this even more clearly . . ."[20] From a psychoanalytic point of view, there is always a question: why does a
person keep coming *back* to something? What is it about the previous attempts that remain both tempting yet unsatisfying—and thus
dictate a return? In this case, why can't Aristotle just say what he
means, be done with it, and move on?[21]

Aristotle seems confident that he can fill in the gap:

> Let us resume our inquiry and state, in view of the fact
> that all knowledge and choice aims at some good, what it
> is that we say political science aims at and what is the high-
> est of goods achievable by action. *Verbally there is very gen-
> eral agreement;* for both the general run of men and people
> of superior refinement say that it is happiness, and identify
> living well and faring well with being happy; but *with re-
> gard to what happiness is they differ,* and the many do not
> give the same account as the wise. For the former think it
> is some plain and obvious thing, like pleasure, wealth, or
> honor; they differ, however, from one another—and
> often even the same man identifies it with different things,
> with health when he is ill, with wealth when he is poor;
> but, conscious of their ignorance, *they admire those who pro-
> claim some great thing that is above their comprehension.* Now
> some thought that apart from these many goods there is
> another wish is good in itself and causes the goodness of all
> these as well. To examine all the opinions that have been
> held would no doubt be somewhat fruitless: it is enough

to examine those that are most prevalent or that seem to have some reason in their favor.[22]

Aristotle, following Socrates and Plato, wants to argue that the value of our values is that they lead to and constitute a happy life. Of course, there is much to be said about this conception of happiness, but rather than follow Aristotle down that interpretive path, I should like to ask a tangential question: what is he doing when he introduces happiness at this point? I shall explore this question at length. But let me say right away that I think that Aristotle is performing a seduction in the psychoanalytic sense of the term.

Obviously, this needs explanation. To understand this claim I need to distinguish, first, a vulgar from a sophisticated sense of seduction; and, second, within the sophisticated sense of seduction, I need to distinguish a manifest from a latent content. By a seduction in the vulgar sense I mean the flagrant sexual intrusions which Freud, before 1897, thought neurotics had been subjected to in childhood and had repressed.[23] Although Freud abandoned the so-called seduction theory, a number of psychoanalytic thinkers have tried to refine that theory rather than abandon it, in the hope of holding on to a more sophisticated truth.[24] In this more properly psychoanalytic account of seduction, there is recognition that even in healthy relationships between parents and child there are transmissions of unconscious messages. These are experienced as messages but they are necessarily enigmatic. Precisely because these messages escape our understanding, they captivate us: and this moment of captivation is, from a psychoanalytic point of

view, inevitable. In this sophisticated sense, seducti'
tive of our entry into language.

Basically, we have just seen the manifest content of seu...
We are, by our natures, susceptible to enigmatic signifiers—
oracular utterances, if you will—which we can recognize as having a meaning—indeed, as having a special meaning *for us*—but
whose content we do not understand. But the latent content of
seduction is the idea that there is an explanatory end-of-the-line,
an Archimedean point of explanation beyond which one does not
need to go. Freud originally thought that he could stop his explan-
atory-analytic quest when he traced a neurotic's story back to a
real-life seduction. It was as though the simple appeal to reality—
this reality could be the explanatory end of the line. It was here,
Freud thought, that the restless mind that searches for explana-
tions can come to rest.

In abandoning the seduction hypothesis, Freud did not abandon the idea that children were often seduced or abused, nor did
he abandon the hypothesis that such seduction caused serious psychological harm. What he abandoned—at least, according to his
own conscious understanding—was the idea that this happened
always and everywhere in the causation of neurosis. The deeper
idea, though, is the recognition that mind is always active. In particular, it is always active in the creation of fantasies. Thus even
when there is a real-life, flagrant seduction, there is still a further
question: what did the mind do with it? The recognition that
mind is active in producing fantasies of seduction is tantamount to
the admission that there is no Archimedean point, no explanatory
end-of-the-line in a brute appeal to reality.[25]

We are now in a position to call Aristotle a seducer. He injects a special use of an enigmatic signifier into our lives, and he puts it forward as something which ought to be an explanatory end-of-the-line. *Verbally,* Aristotle says, there is very general agreement that *the* good is "happiness," but there is widespread disagreement about what happiness is. The agreement, then, seems only about a word—and about the place such a concept would hold in our lives, if only we could give it content. There is thus also general agreement that this would be a justificatory end-of-the line, but there is at the same time a recognition that no one can say with confidence what this valuable condition consists in.

This seems to be the point of ethical reflection. The injection of "happiness" here does capture our attention. We seem to be seeking "*the* good," and we are on a path of inquiry which we already recognize as attractive to us, but we do not yet have a clear idea of what this attraction is. Aristotle has already said that *if* we had knowledge of the good, that knowledge would have a great influence on our lives. We can recognize now, before we have it, that we would be much better off with this knowledge than without it. He now identifies this good with our happiness: something we can recognize as an ultimate good before we really know what it is. Doesn't this heighten anticipation, exert *some pressure* on us to know? If we are creatures who desire our own happiness, and if happiness is attainable only through rational action (that is why animals cannot be said to be happy), then the injection of the idea that we can consider the happiness of our lives *taken as a whole* must serve to make us discontented. Even the virtuous person will feel, as Aristotle would put it, the "right amount" of discontent. For once this idea of happiness has been introduced it must, as Aristotle himself recognizes, instill a longing to find out what it is.

Aristotle distinguishes the judgment of the many from the judgment of the wise. Now if we again remember the gift of the twentieth century to philosophy —the insight that there can be no fundamental gap between the content of our concepts and the life we live with them—it becomes clear that the use of "the many" cannot simply be a mistake about happiness. It must reveal something about the content of the concept of happiness. The use of "the many" reveals, first, that "happiness" is systematically inconstant. People use it to designate what they don't yet have, what they are longing for, that which they have just lost and would like again. People tend to fantasize that if they just had this missing thing, it would make them happy. Thus, as Aristotle points out, the sick man longs for health and thinks that if only he can be healthy again he would be happy. In his sickness, he is oblivious to the thought that it would be a sign of his regaining health that he turns his attention to something else that is missing and begins to fantasize that it would give him happiness.

Now there is supposedly a perspective—the perspective of "the wise"—from which one can see the fantastic nature of this longing. Nevertheless, the use of "happiness" is irretrievably entangled in that fantasy. Happiness is that which we would attain if our deepest longings (of the moment) were satisfied.

Second, the use of "the many" reveals that they are to some extent aware of their ignorance. "They admire those who proclaim some great things above their comprehension." The many are ready to fall in love with a pronouncement they do not understand. It seems to be intrinsic to our use of the concept of happiness that we are especially vulnerable to seductions invoking it.

But these features of the use of "the many" suggest that "happiness" is a perfect transference concept. It is a blank which holds a place for "that which would satisfy our deepest longings" (whatever they happen to be). Thus, in retrospect, one can see how Aristotle could use the concept to carry out a seduction. Aristotle asks, what is *the* good of all our actions? It seems that we have somehow to take our lives as a whole into account, to do so while we are still in the midst of living and somehow to answer what to do next on the basis of that consideration. There is no obvious way to do this. In effect, Aristotle takes the concept of happiness from its unreflective home—where, for instance, we call the rich happy when we are poor, and in general fantasize that if only we could get . . . we would be happy—and places it in a reflective context in which it is not yet clear how it is to be deployed.

This claim requires explanation. Obviously, there had long been speculation and comment on what made for a happy life.[26] What Aristotle is injecting is the idea that we can somehow be sensitive to *the* good—the happiness of our whole lives—in every decision, every action, every practical deliberation. The problem is that we don't yet know what this sensitivity is or what it is that we are supposed to be sensitive to. In effect, there is an enigmatic signifier already circulating in the population—our "happiness"—and Aristotle, following Socrates and Plato, tries to inject a new use. The idea that there is a special use of "the wise" promotes the fantasy that there is already content to the concept, but that it is perceptible only to those who are in the know. The seductive suggestion is that a very special, esoteric knowledge is needed. This is just how it looks when an enigmatic signifier is introduced: it will look as though there is something mysterious and enticing, and, if only we could get behind the veil, our lives would be, well, . . . happy!

Aristotle now purports to fill in the blank. The good of each activity, he says, is "that for whose sake everything else is done." So "if there is an end for all that we do, this will be the good achievable by action."[27] Aristotle says that he is going to state "even more clearly" what this good is—and he does go through the motions of giving its marks and features—but there is an important sense in which he says nothing. Consider, first, Aristotle's claim that the good is complete.

> Since there are evidently more than one end, and we choose some of these (e.g. wealth, flutes and in general instruments) for the sake of something else, clearly not all ends are complete ends; but *the chief good is evidently something complete.* Therefore if there is only one complete end, this will be what we are seeking, and if there are more than one, the most complete of these will be what we are seeking. Now we call that which is in itself worthy of pursuit more complete than that which is worthy of pursuit for the sake of something else, and that which is never desirable for the sake of something else more complete than the things that are desirable both in themselves and for the sake of that other thing, and therefore we call

complete without qualification [ἁπλῶς δή τέλειον] that which is always desirable in itself and never for the sake of something else.[28]

Aristotle does not here tell us anything about what happiness is actually like. To say that the chief good is complete is basically to utter a tautology. It secures the logical space of an enigmatic signifier: something that holds the place for "the end of desire as such." But this laying out of the logic of an enigmatic signifier tends to obscure the fact that this space is itself created. For there is some sense in which Aristotle's fundamental claim is false: we do "choose" happiness for the sake of being able to live a life in which we conceive of it as forming a coherent whole. This "choice" isn't made, so to speak, inside life: it is, rather, the kind of inaugurating instantiation which gives life an inside. Once we have installed the idea of there being an end of all the things we do, life will thereby be so transformed that it will appear that there is (and always has been) such thing as *a life* having its own possible coherence and end. It will then appear that all possible choices occur in this field: within the context of a life. This is an indication that we have already been seduced into a certain way of life, a way of life that has been structured by the introduction of an enigmatic signifier into it.

Aristotle makes a similar move with the idea that happiness is self-sufficient:

From the point of view of self-sufficiency the same result seems to follow; for the complete good is thought to be self-sufficient . . . *the self-sufficient we now define as that*

which when isolated makes life desirable and lacking in nothing;
and such we think happiness to be; and further we think it
most desirable of all things, without being counted as one
good among others . . .[29]

One should read this, I think, as the utterance of a fantastic tautology: the imagining of the logical space that happiness would have
to occupy. Happiness is that—whatever it is—which makes life
desirable and lacking in nothing. That is, happiness is that, whatever it is, which makes us happy.[30] Now, why do I call this tautology fantastic? Because although it is possible to make perfectly
good sense of this claim, one can also see, just below the surface,
the stirrings of a wish. After all, why formulate the condition of
self-sufficiency in terms of a life *lacking in nothing?* It is a condition
of life that we live with desires—and the experience of desire is
the experience of a certain kind of lack. In a happy life, presumably, we have the right sorts of lacks and are able to satisfy them in
the right sorts of ways. But to characterize such a condition as a
life lacking in nothing hints at the idea that the truly happy life is
somehow beyond lacks—that is, beyond desire. The hint is of a
life which is beyond the exigencies and pressures of life itself. The
fantasy of a happy life becomes tinged with the suggestion of a life
beyond life—a certain kind of living death. I shall return to this.

Aristotle himself seems to recognize that he has not yet said
anything substantial: "Presumably, however, to say that happiness
is the chief good seems a platitude and a clearer account of what it is
still desired. This might perhaps be given if we could first ascertain
the function of man."[31] What the translator calls a "platitude" is

ὁμολογούμενόν τι: strictly, "a certain same-saying." I do not think it a stretch to translate Aristotle thus: "to say that happiness is the chief good seems a tautology." ("Tautology" literally means a same-saying.) Aristotle himself recognizes that he is not making substantial claims either about happiness or the good but is rather laying out the structure of a certain kind of concern. This isn't simply a platitude, nor is it simply something that is agreed upon (another possible translation): it is rather the delineation of the logical space that any candidate for the title "happiness" would have to occupy. But he has not yet said anything about the occupant.

Now when Aristotle at last comes to his famous argument about the function of man, it looks as though he might at last be adding some content to the idea of happiness. But appearances can be deceiving.

> There remains, then, an active life of the element that has a rational principle . . . Now if the function of man is an activity of soul in accordance with, or not without, rational principle . . . the human good turns out to be activity of soul in conformity with excellence, and if there are more than one excellence, in conformity with the best and most complete.[32]

Hasn't Aristotle at last given us the content of happiness? I don't think so. Nothing of substance is added by bringing in the idea of rational activity. "Happiness" is the placeholder for the object of our concern when we take our whole lives into account (whatever it might be to do that). The rational principle here is nothing other than the intelligent, mind-directed approach to happiness (whatever that might be). But that is only to stake out the conceptual field in which happiness is placed. Aristotle himself says that we do not consider any of the other animals happy.[33] This is not because they are psychologically incapable of it, but because the concept has been introduced as the goal of a thoughtful approach to living well, taken as a whole. Again, Aristotle is doing nothing more than locating the place in which the enigmatic signifier must operate.

"But we must add," says Aristotle, "'in a complete life.' For one swallow does not make a summer, nor does one day; and so too one day, or a short time, does not make a man blessed and happy."[34] This is the real transformation: the injecting of a concept into life that purportedly stands to our whole life as the good stands to any activity within that life. It should not be surprising, therefore, that the introduction of this concept raises conceptual problems that Aristotle has difficulty resolving.[35] Can we call no man happy while he is alive? This is not just a matter of clearing up confusions or brushing away sophistries. The injection of an enigmatic signifier carries with it the possibilities of contradictions, unworked-out problems.

Is it only the dead we can call happy, Aristotle asks, as being beyond misfortunes and reversals? But, he goes on, that would be absurd, because we consider happiness to be an activity. And yet, he continues, "it is odd that when he is happy the attribute that belongs to him is not to be truly predicated of him because we do not wish to call living men happy, on account of the changes that might befall them."[36] This is a serious problem for Aristotle—and he has no real answer. He does offer certain empirical consolations: that the virtues are the best way to keep one's balance when misfortune threatens and that, even in misfortune, one can never become base. But there is no conceptual clarification. And this would suggest that there is no answer: it would suggest, that is, that we are not here dealing with an articulated concept known only to "the wise" but with an enigmatic signifier.

Aristotle even manages to get himself puzzled about how far the concept of happiness extends: can a person's happiness be affected after he is dead? The familiar point made by commentators is that the Greek conception of happiness is not coincident with our own. The less familiar point is that this "concept" is not tied down. Notice how tentative Aristotle is:

> That the fortunes of descendants and of all a man's friends should not affect his happiness at all seems a very unfriendly doctrine, and one opposed to the opinions men hold . . . and it makes a difference whether the various sufferings befall the living or the dead . . . or rather, perhaps, the fact that doubt is felt whether the dead share in any good or evil. For it seems, from these considerations, that even if anything whether good or evil penetrates to them, it must be something weak and negligible . . . at least it must be such in degree and kind as not to make happy those who are not happy nor take away their blessedness from those who are. The good and bad fortunes of friends, then seem to have some effects on the dead, but effects of such a kind and degree as neither to make the happy unhappy nor to produce any other change of kind.[37]

Now it may seem "unfriendly" to hold that the misfortunes of loved ones will in no way affect the recently dead, but who says death is friendly to our wishes? Again, this may run counter to the opinions of most people, but is there any topic about which one should have less confidence in "the many" than in their beliefs about what happens after death? Aristotle cannot here be trying to get to the truth about happiness. At best, he can be working out the content of common belief. Aristotle does in general think one should consult common opinion—for *about features in this world* people do tend to grab onto some aspect of reality, even if they do so in a distorted form. But it is obvious that about life after death, "the many" know nothing. In consulting common opinion on this subject one learns about cultural myths and fantasies; the many have fantasies, but they know nothing about the happiness of the dead. But this is all right if Aristotle is not trying to find out the truth about happiness, but is facilitating a seduction. For he is taking powerful and widely held wishes about happiness and claiming that these wishes can legitimately attach to the enigmatic signifier he is introducing.

Aristotle goes through the motions of "testing" his argument against common beliefs: "We must consider it, however, in the light not only of our conclusion and our premises, but also of what is commonly said about it: for with a true view all the facts harmonize, but with a false one they soon clash."[38] On the surface this looks like a kind of empirical confirmation, testing one's position in the light of hypotheses that others hold. However, when it comes to popular beliefs, we have seen that Aristotle has already cut his cloth to fit current fashion. For the rest, he does no more than locate the logical space in which this enigmatic signifier is placed. Aristotle admits as much himself: "we have practically defined happiness as a sort of living and faring well."[39] Similarly with the claims that it is a kind of excellence, that it is itself pleasant and among the most godlike things.[40] Thus far we know practically nothing about happiness. But, ironically, knowing practically nothing is essential to the seduction.[41]

Aristotle's remarks thus far have all the hallmarks of an interpretation—at least, according to one understanding of that term. It looks as though Aristotle is saying to his audience, "Look, this is what your life was already about. You might not have consciously understood that you were aiming toward happiness, but now that I've given you this interpretation you can take better practical hold of your lives." Thus it looks as though Aristotle is just passing on to us a piece of knowledge—something which was already true but about which we were ignorant. That is precisely what an inaugurating instantiation will look like—*if* it is successful. Aristotle has already said that reflective understanding of *the* good will change our lives in important ways. But from the perspective of the later Wittgenstein and Heidegger, there is no coherent way to understand the idea of changing our lives with a concept in fundamental ways while holding the content of that concept constant.

In fact, it is arguable that Aristotle is striving for nothing less than an ontological transformation of human being. To see this, let us start with Heidegger's idea that we are ontologically constituted by care. To see that this is more than a deep psychological fact about us, consider the following counterfactual schema:

If we were to cease to care, then . . .

The point is not that all counterfactuals of such form are false, but that they are all nonsensical.[42] We see this when we recognize that the antecedent is not specifying any coherent condition. In the closest condition in which we cease to care, "we" cease to be. No doubt, one can find human beings in psychiatric institutions in severe catatonic states, in massive autistic enclosedness, where it does make sense to say that they have ceased to care. But precisely in looking at this allegedly limiting case we can see what is at stake: in ceasing to care, they have ceased to be one of us. This is not to draw a line between one tribe and another, one culture and another; it is to gesture in the direction of what it is to fall out of human being. The "fact" that we care, then, is not simply an important fact about what we are like; it is a structuring condition of the universe of our possibilities.

Now it seems that Aristotle is trying to get us to recognize that we are in a similar position with respect to.

If we were to cease to care-about-our-happiness, then . . .

First, Aristotle insists that humans are the only animals capable of happiness. Other creatures may flourish in their distinctive ways, but only humans can be concerned about their happiness—and this concern seems to be a constitutive condition of happiness itself.[43] It seems that Aristotle is here trying to make an ontological distinction: he is mapping out the realm of human being. Second,

Aristotle explicitly sees *all* forms of human being as various types of carings-about-happiness. Indeed, for Aristotle, one differentiates among these forms of being not in terms of whether there is a concern for happiness or not, but in terms of what form that concern takes. The virtuous person, for example, is harmoniously motivated in ways that accurately express and promote his happiness. Among people who suffer conflicts, Aristotle recognizes two types. First, there is the "continent" person, who feels a conflict but in the end manages to do the right thing. Second, there is the "incontinent" (or *akratic*) who decides to do one thing but then acts against his best judgment. This is Aristotle's model of an irrational act. But in the cases of both the "continent" and "incontinent" persons, their conflicts are among things they take to be goods. Temptation is the paradigm occasion for conflict, but whether or not one gives in, both sides of the conflict are directed toward some image of happiness. The wicked or intemperate person is the mirror image of virtue: he is pursuing some bad end—but only because he (mistakenly) believes it will promote his happiness. In short, for Aristotle, all forms of human being are structured by this concern.

The apparent universality of this concern helps Aristotle remain unaware of his ontological sleight of hand. For by introducing the idea that we are ontologically constituted by a concern for our happiness, he in effect slips in the idea that we are ontologically constituted by a concern for our lives *as a whole*. This does seem an unconscious attempt at making-true. For it is precisely the concern for our lives as a whole which serves to make our lives whole. And it is by introducing "happiness" as a way we might evaluate our lives as a whole, as a purported evaluative frame for our current understanding of what we are doing here and now, that life gets to be constituted as a whole. And insofar as Aristotle takes concern-for-our-happiness to structure all the possibilities of human being, he has endeavored to change our ontological constitution without noticing that that is what he is doing.

That, it seems to me, is the unconscious aim of Greek ethical reflection: to change our ontology without our noticing it. Thus we see the power of a certain form of interpretation: not just to change life, but to change the structure of possibilities in which life can be lived.

In analysis, we are always interested when the analysand makes a sudden shift. And there is no doubt but that there is an abrupt shift in the last few pages of the *Nicomachean Ethics*—a shift which changes the meaning of the book as a whole. Had those pages not been there, the obvious lesson of the book would be that the happy life is the active life of the traditional ethical virtues informed by practical wisdom. But Aristotle famously closes the *Ethics* by claiming that in fact such a life would provide only "second-rate happiness."[44] The truly happy life is contemplative.

Generations of scholars have reacted in one of two ways. First, they have tried to show that the appearance of a shift is only an appearance. They point to hints earlier in the text and argue that contemplation is the direction in which Aristotle has been moving all along.[45] Second, philosophers who are interested in the contemporary value of an Aristotelian approach to ethics tend to discount the end of the book, treating it as part of Aristotle's theology—of historical interest but not relevant to the central ethical approach of the book. These philosophers focus on Aristotle's account of how virtues are instilled by habit and how they bestow their own distinctive ways of seeing and reacting to situations.

I don't want to move in either direction, for both seem to me to be the work of philosophy's ego. Not that I have anything against the ego per se. It *is* of value to show an underlying unity to the *Nicomachean Ethics* taken as a whole. But it is precisely the ingenuity of displaying this underlying unity which covers over the strain in doing so. Similarly, it is of course of value to use Aristotle as inspiration for contemporary approaches to ethics, but the beauty and excitement of that activity covers over the violence involved in lopping off a significant section of the book.

I should therefore like to try a change of tack. Leaving aside the question of the ultimate coherence or incoherence, I want to stay closer to the surface of the text and ask: what is the effect of this *apparent* disruption? What is involved in this last-minute recognition that the truly happy life is the contemplative one? The answer seems to me surprising. Just below the surface of the familiar arguments, the text serves to promote discontent and to valorize death.

If the *Nicomachean Ethics* had ended at book X chapter 6, the opening lines of the text would, in retrospect, look like a come-on. Why, after all, would we need an image of archers given a distant mark to aim at if the upshot of ethical reflection is that the life that we are already living is the happy one? The metaphor would be wildly off. A more appropriate metaphor would be the adding of a bit of mortar between the already-secure bricks of the solid edifice. But the introduction of the ideal of a contemplative life does at last give us a mark to aim at, for it does involve a shifting of sights onto that mark. At the last minute, we are encouraged to think differently about the lives we are already leading.

The shift is in our conception of what it is about our lives that really gives it value. And this will lead to a restructuring of our lives. Not that the contemplative life is altogether different from the practical life, but now that large part of life which is engaged in practical activity will be understood from inside that life as aiming toward the contemplative life.[46] That is, such a practical life, *when it succeeds in its project,* will be a contemplative life. For a contemplative life is not one in which we are always contemplating. Rather, what makes the life contemplative is, first, that practical life itself is understood as organized for the sake of providing time and space for contemplative activity; second, the practical activity of life is actually successful in securing room for contemplation; third, it is understood that it is this contemplative activity which gives this life its deepest value. The move from a practical to a contemplative life will involve a rethinking of the value and organization of practical life.

It is crucial to Aristotle's restructuring of ethical life that "happiness" has been functioning for him as an enigmatic signifier. He begins:

If happiness is activity in accordance with excellence, it is reasonable that it should be in accordance with the highest excellence; and this will be that of the best thing in us. Whether it be intellect or something else that is this element which is thought to be our natural ruler and guide and to take thought of things noble and divine, whether it be itself also divine or only the most divine element in us, the activity of this in accordance with its proper excellence will be complete happiness. That this activity is contemplative we have already said.[47]

Aristotle seems to be pursuing a thought to its logical conclusion, but note that this is possible because we do not yet know what happiness is. It has been introduced as a standard, yet because it is enigmatic we are susceptible to a last-minute shift in understanding what the point of our lives might be. It is the ethical equivalent of receiving an oracle and only at the last minute coming to understand its meaning *for us*. Aristotle, of course, relies here on an overall teleological framework, and he appeals to "the best thing in us." The effect though must be to set us at a distance from happiness. For let us just suppose that we are the intended audience for these lectures: we are already well brought up, mature, more or less leading an ethically virtuous life and are now following Aristotle in a reflection on that life. Until this moment we ought to have been thinking that we are already living happy lives; but now comes the moment of separation. We begin to realize that the lives we have been living are not *completely* happy. So, although we are at this moment the furthest away from "the many's" conception of happiness, this highest conception of happiness does have something in common with the lowest: we are again conceiving happiness as what we don't at the moment have. Aristotle will achieve this distance by retrospectively giving new content to what is meant by "complete happiness." And because we have already been seduced by the enigmatic nature of this signifier, there is pressure to go along.

Aristotle now argues that whatever the hallmarks of happiness are, one gets more of them in a contemplative life. Contemplative activity is, he says, more "continuous" and "self-sufficient" than ordinary practical activity.

And the self-sufficiency spoken of must belong most to the contemplative activity. For while a wise man, as well as a just man and the rest, needs the necessaries of life, when they are sufficiently equipped with things of that sort the just man needs people towards whom and with whom he shall act justly, and the temperate man and the brave man and each of the others is in the same case, but the wise man, even when by himself, can contemplate truth, and the better the wiser he is; he can perhaps do so better if he has fellow workers, but still he is the most self-sufficient. And *this activity alone would seem to be loved for its own sake; for nothing arises from it apart from the contemplating, while from practical activities we gain more or less apart from the action. And happiness is thought to depend on leisure; for we are busy that we may have leisure, and make war that we may live in peace.* Now the activity of the practical excellences is exhibited in political or military affairs, but the actions concerned with these seem to be unleisurely.

Warlike actions are completely so (for no one chooses to be at war, or provokes war for the sake of being at war; *any one would seem absolutely murderous if he were to make enemies of his friends in order to bring about battle and slaughter;*) but *the action of the statesman is also unleisurely,* and—apart from the political action itself—aims at despotic power and honors, or at all events happiness, for him and his fellow citizens—*a happiness different from political action and evidently sought as being different.* So if among excellent actions political and military actions are distinguished by nobility and greatness, and these are unleisurely and aim at an end and are not desirable for their own sake, but the activity of intellect which is contemplative, seems both to be superior in worth and to aim at no end beyond itself, and to have its pleasure proper to itself (and this augments the activity), and *the self-sufficiency, lesisureliness, unweariedness (so far as this is possible for man), and all the other attributes ascribed to the blessed man are evidently those connected with this activity, it follows that this will be the complete happiness of man, if it be allowed a complete term of life* (for none of the attributes of happiness is incomplete).[48]

As an empirical claim, it is dubious that the contemplative man needs others less, for he needs society to make possible the conditions of leisure in which he can contemplate. But as a logical point, the just man necessarily acts in relation to others; the contemplative man acts on his own. What matters for us is the shift in value toward this solitary activity, for it represents a shift away from the idea that the exercise of the ethical virtues is its own reward. The practical virtues are now said to offer some level of gain apart from themselves. And this, in effect, opens up a possibility for discontent within an ethically virtuous life. Had Aristotle not formulated the theoretical difference between practical and impractical activity, there would be no room for this discontent. But once contemplation is isolated from other forms of mental activity, the thought becomes available that only it is loved for its own sake, for nothing arises from it other than itself. Aristotle is now filling in a meaning for the enigmatic "self-sufficient." If we have been following Aristotle step by step, we already committed ourselves at the beginning of the inquiry to the idea that "happiness" is "self-sufficient." This is, as it were, our ethical oracle. Now, in the closing pages of the *Ethics*, we purportedly find out what we have all along been committed to. Quite literally, we find out what the meaning of our life ought to be. And, at the same moment, most of us will discover that our lives fall short.

In this way, valorizing the contemplative ideal is tantamount to introducing a source of discontent within ethical life. We were lured into ethical reflection by the promise of a distant mark which, as archers, we could aim at. And, true to his word, Aristotle does give us a mark by which we might reorient our sense of an excellent life. But this suggests that the practical virtues themselves encourage a reflection that ultimately leads to the conclusion that they are there for the sake of something beyond themselves. In other words, the life of practical virtue has within itself the possibility for generating its own sense of discontent.

For this reason, the *Nicomachean Ethics* is not as complacent a document as it is often taken to be. It is by now a familiar claim that Aristotle's ethics articulates the values of an aristocratic class; and while this may be true, it overlooks the discontent that is being built into the outlook. So, for example, the point is often made that the theorist of masters will of course valorize leisure—and the activities that can be carried out only in leisure time. This may be an accurate political criticism, but from a psychoanalytic point of view, life itself tends to be experienced in terms of various forms of pressure. According to Freud, the very first forms of mental activity—the hallucination of the absent breast under conditions of rising tension—is a fantasy of what it would take to be released from this pressure. Human-mindedness, at its heart, is constituted by various fantasies of release from the pressure of life. In effect, Aristotle takes up this longing and tries to incorporate it into a teleological framework. Nonleisured, busy activity is now interpreted as for the sake of leisure. This introduces a source of discontent with the nonleisured life—and it does so by structuring a fantasy. What had hitherto been experienced as the contentless pressure of practical life is now explained as that from which we would be released if only we could attain a contemplative state.

To be sure, Aristotle does say that the life of practical virtue is a happy one. But one does not understand that life properly, nor does one live it properly, unless one experiences it as pointed toward contemplation. That is, if one does not understand one's life as so oriented, one cannot attain the highest form of happiness—at best, there is second-rate happiness. But as soon as one does understand one's life in this way, there is also the recognition that, most likely, this second-rate happiness is as good as it gets. The political life at its highest does have a certain nobility, but once this higher form of happiness has been introduced, the political life is seen as aiming beyond itself. This is an example of how one can become ensnared in enigmatic signifiers. At the beginning of the inquiry we were invited to agree that "happiness" was "complete" and "self-sufficient" though we had little understanding of what any of these terms might mean. They seemed together to articulate a logical structure of teleological striving. But now a new conception of happiness is introduced in relation to which the political life, even at its best, is now revealed as "incomplete," as not *really* "self-sufficient."

Aristotle is explicit that now that the vista of a contemplative life has opened up, the life of practical virtue now appears "second rate":

> But in a secondary degree the life in accordance with the other kind of excellence is happy; for the activities in accordance with this befit our human estate. Just and brave acts, and other excellent acts, we do in relation to each other, observing what is proper to each with regard to contracts and services and all manner of actions with regard to passions; and all of these seem to be human . . . The excellence of the intellect is a thing apart; we must be content to say this much about it, for to describe it precisely is a task greater than our purpose requires. It would seem, however, also to need external equipment but little, or less than moral excellence does . . . The liberal

man will need money for the doing of his liberal deeds, and the just man too will need it for the returning of services (for wishes are hard to discern, and even people who are not just pretend to wish to act justly); and the brave man will need power if he is to accomplish any of the acts that correspond to his excellence, and the temperate man will need opportunity; for how else is either he or any of the others to be recognized? . . . for deeds many things are needed, and more the greater and nobler the deeds are. But the man who is contemplating the truth needs no such thing, at least with a view to the exercise of his activity . . .

But that *complete happiness is a contemplative activity* will appear from the following consideration as well. We assume the gods to be above all other beings blessed and happy; but what sort of actions must we assign to them? Acts of justice? Will not the gods seem absurd if they make contracts and return deposits, and so on? Acts of a brave man, then confronting dangers and running risks because it is noble to do so? Or liberal acts? To whom will they give? It will be strange if they are really to have money or anything of the kind. And what would their temperate acts be? Is not such praise tasteless, since they have no bad appetites? If we were to run through them all, the circumstances of action would be found trivial and unworthy of gods. Still every one supposes that they *live* and therefore that they are active; we cannot suppose them to sleep like Endymion. Now if you take away from a living being action, and still more production, what is left but

contemplation? Therefore the activity of God, which sur-
passes all others in blessedness, must be contemplative,
therefore that which is most akin to this must be most the
nature of happiness.[49]

If one looks at the overall movement of thought (and emotion)
from the beginning of the *Nicomachean Ethics* up until this moment, one can see the structure of a trauma. According to Freud,
trauma has a retrospective structure.[50] In the typical scenario that
Freud first envisaged, a child has an experience—a seduction—
that at the time she cannot understand. Nevertheless, a trace of
the event is laid down in memory. Only later, as the child develops, is there an experience that triggers a retrospective understanding of the meaning of the earlier experience. But this new
understanding cannot be assimilated: it wounds the mind that
was on the verge of understanding it. On this model, neither of
the two experiences is traumatic in and of itself. The earlier experience need not have been traumatic when it occurred, because it was registered but not understood. The later experience,
for its part, can be innocent in itself—as, for instance, the experience of mild sexual arousal in a situation that triggers a reminis-
cence of the earlier occasion. What becomes explosive is the
cocktail of both those experiences.

Now the beginning of the *Nicomachean Ethics* is like the stage
of childhood seduction. Ethically speaking, we are children when
we begin. As the intended audience, we have been well brought
up and are, so to speak, well disposed toward virtue. But we do
not yet understand the meaning of our ethical habits and disposi-

tions. We do not yet really understand our own character. In this sense, the *Nicomachean Ethics* is the beginning of an ethical reflection on who we are. It is at this point that Aristotle installs a number of enigmatic messages to us: that our lives as a whole are directed toward "happiness," that there is "*the* good," "the end of all the things we do," and that happiness is "complete" and "self-sufficient." There is no way at the beginning of inquiry that we can understand what these messages mean. And thus they must have a certain oracular appeal for us, drawing us into this inquiry, yet puzzling and intriguing us.

The bulk of the book is then taken up with an exploration of the ethical life—the life organized around and giving expression to the traditional ethical virtues. Aristotle sometimes calls this the "political life" because the highest expression of such a life would be that of the statesman organizing, legislating, and running the polis. This is our ethical adolescence. And it is here that the trauma occurs. Aristotle said in book I that the proper statesman would have to have his eye on *the* good, for it is his job to organize the polis so as to promote it. Indeed, as we have seen, Aristotle rather preposterously claims that we should look to the actual activities of statesmen to get some idea of what he means by "*the* good." But if the highest expression of ethical life is the statesman actually legislating for *the* good, he has to know what he is legislating for. And it is at this point of reflection that ethical life suffers a trauma. For we find that the "meanings" laid down in ethical childhood come to acquire meaning in the course of ethical development that the ethical life can no longer contain.

Aristotle has seduced us into discontent with the ethical life as such. It is now seen as yielding, at best, a kind of "second-rate" happiness. This is what Freud would call a compromise formation. We are told that the ethical life is still a happy one, but there is now a discontent-inducing qualification. At the beginning of the *Ethics,* as he delineates the marks and features of "happiness," Aristotle says, "but we must add: in a complete life"—and he takes up the problem of reversals and misfortunes in life. The consolation he offered was that the virtuous person was the best equipped to keep his balance—he better than anyone else would be able to tolerate the reversal without losing his happiness. But now what we have at the end of the *Ethics* is a kind of intellectual reversal. If the ethically virtuous person really is good at keeping his balance, then he ought to take this occasion to shift his life from an ethical life to a contemplative one. If he cannot do so, he will be able to retain his happiness, but he cannot help but realize that it is second-rate.

In effect, Aristotle is recommending a different level of homeostasis for the best human life. That is, instead of living one's entire life at the level of a practical engagement with the world, that engagement should now be seen as aiming at producing a surplus that makes leisure possible—and thus makes possible the activities appropriate to leisure. This transformation, in which practical activity is now seen as aiming beyond itself, turns practical activity into busy-ness. Again, it is familiar to give a political critique of this move: a theorist of the master class will try to valorize leisure activity. But from a psychoanalytic point of view, there is a deeper, inchoate urge which is getting expressed in a specific formulation. Psychoanalytically speaking, any form of life will tend to generate a fantasy of what it is to get outside that life. This is because life is experienced, consciously and unconsciously, as being lived under pressure—and it is correlative to that experience that there is a fantasy of release. Thus it is to be expected that as soon as ethical life gets conceptualized as such—as soon as we can experience such a life as forming *a life*—there will tend to be fantasies about what it would be like *to get outside*. Aristotle formulates a specific instance of such a fantasy, filling it out in teleological and aristocratic terms, but the fantasy has the general structure of promising true happiness just outside the "confines" in which we ordinarily live. In this sense, "the wise" have returned at a theoretical level to the view of "the many." The many, you will recall, thought, when they were sick, that happiness lay in health, and when they were poor that happiness lay in wealth. Now we find that the ethically virtuous think that *real* happiness lies in contemplation.

The idea of a contemplative life is a powerful organizing fantasy—one that tends to hide its fantastic status. After all, one might think, the contemplative life is a real possibility—indeed, Aristotle must have thought that he was living such a life. Why, then, call this a fantasy? This is an important question, and it deserves a layered response. But in the first instance I want to claim that this question itself helps to cover over the fantastic nature of the contemplative life. That is, the very fact that a contemplative life could actually be lived makes it seem as though it is not a fantasy. But the question of whether or not something is a fantasy is not answered by whether one can act on it. Some fantasies one can act on, others not. The real issue is what motivations get organized and expressed by the fantasy. What we need to look at is how life gets reorganized by the insertion into it of the ideal of a contemplative life.

The ideal of a contemplative life involves, as we have already seen, a reorientation of the meaning of that life. Consider an ethically virtuous person, in the midst of his life, who has just sat through Aristotle's lectures—that is, someone who has just got to the point where we are now. What he must realize at the end of the semester that he could not realize at the beginning is that there is now a completely transformed meaning to "in a complete life." At the beginning of the semester he could think: "I am already living a virtuous life. If I can *just* keep this up throughout my life I will have led a complete, happy life. And there is no better guarantee that I will be able to continue to lead such a life other than that I already am leading such a life. Already being virtuous is the best guarantee I could have that I will be able to go on in the same way." But by the end of the semester, he has to think: "If I *only* go on living in this way, I will have achieved at most second-rate happiness." So, a source of discontent has been injected into the ethical life. He now will reorient his life so as to aim for contemplation. Before he achieves the leisure time in which to contemplate, he cannot know with certainty whether the occasion will ever arise. Thus his ethically virtuous life must be lived with a certain amount of hope, expectation and uncertainty. Of course, being virtuous, he will experience these emotions in moderation, but they will be there. And even when he achieves the leisured occasion for contemplation—and experiences the highest form of pleasure and happiness—he must recognize that such occasions as these will be short-lived by comparison to the rest of his life.

To be sure, Aristotle is talking about the happy life. And a contemplative life is a contemplative life even during the stretches within it when one is not contemplating. It is the entire life that is the happiest life. Fine. The real issue, though, is the lived content of this happiest life. Aristotle explicitly says that the lived moments of contemplation are both more pleasant and overall better than the noncontemplative moments of a contemplative life. So even in the best and happiest human life, most of the moments of that life will be lived with the realization that what ultimately makes that life the happiest and the best are passing moments within that life. And even in those best and happiest moments of the best and happiest life there is room for the thought that this is a fleeting part of one's life.

From a psychoanalytic point of view, this is all just as well. If contemplation were a state that one could achieve and sustain indefinitely and unproblematically, then Aristotle would have been led to feel discontent within it—and he would start to fantasize a *real* happiness which lies just outside. The beauty of contemplation as a candidate for occupying a special place of longing is, first, that, for Aristotle, it is the teleologically highest form of activity. Second, it is all but inaccessible for most people, even the ethically virtuous. Third, those few who do manage to find time to contemplate will experience that time as precious and short-lived. As if to drive the point home, Aristotle emphasizes that even if one is living the best and happiest human life, it falls short of the life of the gods, who get to contemplate endlessly and eternally.

But [the contemplative] life would be too high for man;
for it is not in so far as he is man that he will live so, but in
so far as something divine is present in him; and by so
much as this is superior to our composite nature is its activity superior to that which is the exercise of the other
kind of excellence. If intellect is divine, then, in comparison with man, the life according to it is divine in comparison with human life. But we must not follow those
who advise us, being men, to think of human things, and
being mortal, of mortal things, but must, so far as we can,
make ourselves immortal and strain every nerve to live in
accordance with the best thing in us, for even if it be small
in bulk, much more does it in power and worth surpass
everything. This would seem, too, to be each man himself, since it is the authoritative and better part of him. It
would be strange, then, if he were to choose not the life of
himself but that of something else. And what we said before will apply now; that which is proper to each thing is
by nature best and most pleasant for each thing; for man,
therefore, *the life according to intellect is best and pleasantest,
since intellect more than anything else is man. This life therefore
is also the happiest.*[51]

I don't think it takes much imagination to see Aristotle saying
that the happiest life has a smidge of disappointment built into it.
Again there are the two sides of the same message. In contemplating we join in the activity of the gods; in contemplating we fall
short of their activity.[52] That we must "strain every nerve" suggests

it is a real effort to get outside the ordinary conditions of life—even the ethically virtuous life. And in the very process we are reminded of our own mortality. In relation to the gods, we have a sense not only of glorified participation with them (or: do not have a sense only of that) but also of the overwhelming distance that separates our contemplative activities from theirs. In achieving the ultimate human happiness we thereby become aware of the finite and limited nature of that happiness.

There is, though, at least the guarantee that within life we will always have something to strive for. In this way, the contemplative ideal gives meaning and shape to our experiences of discontent. It gives a shape to desire—and a guarantee that we will always stay at a certain distance from the ultimate object of our desire. Thus the basic experience of pressure in being alive is given a certain kind of shape and meaning. It has a shape that promises some escape from the pressure of life, while at the same time ensuring that the fantasy will always be in place to explain the continuing experience of discontent which is life itself.

All this would suggest that Aristotle implicitly recognizes that true human happiness involves keeping happiness at a safe distance. It shouldn't be too far away or we'll get discouraged, but if it gets too close we'll start to feel some discontent with it and fantasize another happiness, lying just beyond the current horizon. And in placing true happiness just beyond the horizon of the ethical life, Aristotle introduces a lack into that life. Something is now experienced as missing from it. So the function of the idea of a contemplative life, from a psychoanalytic point of view, is not, as presented, to give us an end state which when achieved will finally give us true happiness. Rather it is to give us a fantasy for our present use, something we can aim for from a distance. Notice that we began the *Ethics* with Aristotle introducing a gap into ethical life. Ethical reflection is inaugurated with Aristotle's injection of the enigmatic signifier "happiness." An inquiry was then launched into what that "happiness" could be. By the end of the inquiry, though, we close that gap with a gap. The answer to the question "What is happiness?" is that it is a "something" that lies outside the ethical life itself. Now the point of the ethical life is to get outside it. And given that contemplation is praised for being the most solitary and ultimate self-sufficient human activity, it is hard to resist the conclusion that, for Aristotle, *the fundamental good of ethics is to get as far away from your neighbors as possible.* The less you have to do with them the better! Even in the midst of ethical life, its real value, when correctly understood, is that someday it will allow you to get away from it.

But what is this getting away from it all? Looked at from a certain angle, it looks as though Aristotle is valorizing death. At least, among the activities of life, he valorizes the one that comes closest to a fantasy of being in a deathlike state. First, it is an image of an escape from the pressures of ordinary practical life. It is what we would do in our best leisure time, and as such it is the ideal of what one does in a kind of existential Sabbath.[53] It is a higher form of activity than that of the nonleisurely practical life—and thus it is what we would do when we have got beyond life (as it is ordinarily lived). Second, contemplation is the activity of the gods; thus it is in itself a deathless activity. But deathless activity is precisely what the dead do; only the living engage in activities which come to an end. When Aristotle tries to think through what the gods do, he immediately eliminates all practical activities—all the fulfilling of needs or desires, all busywork. But for gods to be gods they must be active: so Aristotle needs to focus on an activity that isn't itself the practical filling of a need. In other words, if you want to hold onto the bare idea of liveliness and activity but take away from that idea as many marks and features of actual life as lived, you end up with contemplation.[54] Contemplation is the most deathlike form of life. Thus it is that, imaginatively speaking, immortality is a form of death; it is what death would be like if death were a form of life. For death is our immortal condition. Note that Aristotle stresses that contemplation is our most "continuous" activity, allowing the least interruption, that it is our most solitary and self-sufficient activity, and that it is complete in and of itself. If death were an activity, it would be like that.

At just this point in the argument, Aristotle reiterates a point he has made earlier: that other animals cannot be happy.[55] These are creatures who cannot take their lives as a whole into account, and thus cannot reason practically about the happiness of their lives. In other words, they cannot take their deaths into account; and their inability to take their death into account is intimately tied to their inability to be happy.

This, I think, sheds light on the value of our values. By this stage of reflection, it seems that, for Aristotle, the value of our reflection on the best life is that it induces a kind of being-unto-death. It creates a fantasy of a release from the ordinary pressures of ethical life, a fantasy of sharing with the gods the greatest, stressless pleasure. This is a fantasy that carries within it an experience of lack, an experience of being at a distance from this wonderful goal. It is a fantasy of release which helps us organize and direct our ordinary practical lives. Those who know most about human life know that what is best is to organize life so as to escape its ordinary conditions—even the conditions of excellence within it. What is best about being human is the opportunity to break out of being human. Or: to be most human is to break out of the ordinary conditions of human life.

If Aristotle were the Aristotle with whom we think we are familiar, one would expect the *Ethics* to end with a summing up of all that has been accomplished in the text. One finds no such thing: "are we to suppose that our program has reached its end? Surely, as is said, where there are things to be done, the end is not to survey and recognize the various things, but rather to do them."[56] In fact, one finds an Aristotle who seems somewhat irritated, saying that the real work is only about to begin.

As book X chapter 8 ends, we are in a position to draw the following conclusions. First, most people are not and will never be happy; second, even the elite who lead an ethically virtuous life achieve only second-rate happiness; third, those few who are able to lead a contemplative life will at best be able to contemplate for relatively short periods of their lives. In brief, happiness by and large eludes the human condition. Humans may long for it in the way they long to win the lottery—and, in fact, the mass of humankind has a better chance of winning the lottery. At least with the lottery every ticket has an equal chance; for the mass of humankind the very possibility of happiness is ruled out at birth (or shortly thereafter). Those who are not lucky enough to be born into a situation in which they can be well brought up have no chance.

All the rest of animal nature is basically able to fulfill its nature unproblematically. There will be occasional mutants and occasions when the environment doesn't cooperate, but for the most part each species is able to flourish in its distinctive way. It is only humans who have a characteristic problem of failing to thrive. For humans, happiness *is* human flourishing, yet happiness by and large eludes them. Thus by injecting "happiness" as the organizing goal of human teleology Aristotle manages to disrupt the teleological structure itself. For he has made it virtually impossible for humans to fulfill their nature. Although the teleological worldview is used to give content to what happiness consists in, once the picture is filled out it puts pressure on the teleological worldview itself.

Aristotle tries to save his teleology by a flight to aristocracy. "The many," he says, are not swayed by good arguments[57]—this is to be expected by now—but Aristotle now suggests that even if they had been brought up under good laws, they would still need to be tightly controlled by law throughout their lives. In other words, it is not simply a matter of their not having been well brought up to begin with. "But it is surely not enough that when they are young they should get the right nurture and attention; since they must, even when they are grown up, practice and be habituated to them, we shall need laws for this as well, and generally speaking to cover the whole of life; for most people obey necessity rather than argument, and punishments rather than what is noble."[58] This is the teleological irony of aristocracy. On the surface it looks like the expression of a teleological worldview that only the best should live in the best way. Yet this position also expresses, as it covers over, an anomaly in the system: namely, that the human race is the only species in nature almost all of whose members are failing to flourish. This disruption of the harmonious order is caused precisely by the introduction of "happiness" as the purported concept by which we should evaluate our lives. It is usually assumed that it is because Aristotle was an aristocrat that he was attracted to such a teleological worldview. The question now arises whether to hold onto his teleology he had to be an aristocrat.

But even the aristocratic ploy no longer seems to be able to contain his doubts:

if (as we have said) *the man who is to be good* must be well trained and habituated, and go on to spend his time in worthy occupations and neither willingly nor unwillingly do bad actions, and if this can be brought about if men live in accordance with a sort of intellect and right order, *provided this has force—if this be so, the paternal command indeed has not the required force or compulsive power* (nor in general has the command of one man, unless he be a king or something similar), but the law *has* compulsive power, while it is at the same time an account proceeding from a sort of practical wisdom and intellect. And while people *hate* men who oppose their impulses, even if they oppose them rightly, *the law in its ordaining of what is good is not burdensome.*[59]

The suggestion here seems to be that the compulsive power of law is needed *even for the good.* One reason is to contain the hatred a son would otherwise feel for his father. According to Aristotle, if a son's impulses were not inhibited by an impersonal law, but by his father's prohibition, the son would come to hate the father. It no longer seems as though happiness is unproblematically available even for those who already are good.

So even those who are constitutionally prepared for happiness, those who have been born into the right circumstances and well brought up—even they would have problems without the law. And yet, the law doesn't yet exist! No one, says Aristotle, has really thought about legislation seriously, and neither politicians nor sophists know what they are talking about.[60] At the beginning of the *Nicomachean Ethics* we were given confidence that *the* good existed by being pointed to political science. The good was purportedly that which legislators legislate. But at the very end of the book this reassurance is taken away. The original appeal was to the actual practice of statesmen in the actual world, but now there is the admission that no one in the actual world knows what he is doing.

From this perspective the beginning of the *Ethics* looks especially seductive. We were lured into a false sense of confidence about *the* good: even if we didn't know what it was, there were purportedly experts—those in the know—and they were the masters of political science. But now that the argument has already secured the conclusion that the truly happy life is contemplative not political, he can kick away the ladder. For him the question now becomes how to formulate legislation for a polis in ways that will keep most people on the right track practically speaking while making room for philosophy among the few.

At this point, a certain question becomes irresistible: Does Aristotle's entire ethical system as it reaches this closing moment finally show itself to be an expression of mourning for Socrates? For in this pessimistic-hopeful vision, society is to be legislated in a way that preserves traditional values but makes room for philosophy instead of killing it off. I shall return to this question in the second lecture.

For the moment, I should like to take stock of where we have been. We began with a hope— and an approach to an ethical system that is at once attractive and self-satisfied. The original hope was that we might expand this character- and psychology-based ethics to include an understanding of the unconscious. But as we start to look at the system from a psychoanalytic point of view, we find that instead of being able to add to it, the system itself starts to fall apart. The *Ethics* presents itself as itself part of a larger teleological system in which everything has its place and everything is in its place. What could be more existentially reassuring than to learn that the ethically virtuous life is the happiest? But now it appears that, for humans to be placed in the teleological order, Aristotle has had to disturb the order in which they have been living. Following Socrates and Plato, Aristotle disturbs the universe by injecting "happiness" as a purported concept in terms of which one's entire life can and should be evaluated. It is only when "happiness" is in place that humans can be said to occupy a place in the teleological order—but the teleological order cannot account for its own inauguration. The establishment of a teleological principle—"happiness"—by which to evaluate human life itself lies beyond the teleological principle.

And while it looks on the surface that "happiness" is a profound organizing principle for human life, just under the surface we begin to see that its injection into life has a profoundly disturbing effect. For although it was originally deployed to show that the ethical life was a happy one, by encouraging us to think about the value of our lives taken as a whole Aristotle creates the conditions in which it is possible to formulate the fantasy of real happiness lying just outside. In this way, "happiness" creates its own discontent. Now, Aristotle is too deep and honest a thinker simply to ignore this pressure, and he tries to contain it within the overall framework of his teleological system. But, as I think I have shown, it just doesn't work. The teleological system cannot contain the expression of discontent and breaking-out which it itself generates. The question then becomes: How should we understand this discontent?

It comes out rather more (neo) Platonic than customary

2

D E A T H

Aristotle concludes the *Nicomachean Ethics* with the realization that the ethical life in itself is second-rate. For a happy life of the first rank, one must use one's practical abilities to attain significant periods of living that lie outside the ethical, and which are marked by total impracticality. Aristotle tries to justify this conclusion by appeal to teleology: he ostensibly rests his claim on the idea that contemplation is a *higher* form of activity than the exercise of the ethical virtues. But, as we have seen, the argument bends Aristotle's teleological system out of shape. Nevertheless, it seems to me that there is something profoundly right about Aristotle's conclusion—though Aristotle is not himself in a position to explain why.

Here I am going to attempt an explanation, and you may not be surprised to learn that I am going to appeal to psychoanalytic ideas. What you should be surprised to discover, though, for it certainly surprised me, is that in trying to answer this question, psychoanalysis reveals itself in a foundational crisis. In 1920 Freud opened up a gaping hole in psychoanalysis and then promptly covered it over. He called that covering over "the death drive." Since that time commentary has divided into those who dismiss the death drive as groundless metaphysical speculation and those who think that, in the death drive, Freud saw something profound about the workings of the human mind. If one had to choose, I would be in the latter camp. But I don't think one should have to choose. Even those who take the death drive seriously ought to recognize that the very activity of taking the death drive seriously is a resistance. It is a resistance to seeing a trauma at the core of psychoanalytic theory. In short, there is no such thing as the death drive.

So today we shall move from happiness to death. This is actually a well-worn route, and better philosophers than I have walked it. They, though, have got to the immortality of the soul, and I can assure you I will not get us there.

If one wants to know what it is about the ethical virtues that make a life of them second-rate, one ought to look at what it is about them that makes them attractive. From a contemporary perspective what commands our respect is, first, the seriousness of Aristotle's attempt to ground ethical life in a realistic understanding of human psychology; second, his insistence that ethical life cannot be based on a rule book. A courageous person, for instance, is sensitive and responsive to what, in any particular circumstances, is the courageous thing to do. And there is no authority independent of the judgment of a courageous person—say, a fixed moral code—which could explain or justify that judgment. As Socrates showed, any attempt to lay down what courage is by prescribing particular rules—like standing fast in front of the enemy—will admit of obvious counterexamples—times when it is foolhardy so to act. In this sense, an ethical virtue like courage is *essentially uncodifiable*.

The only way into the courageous life is via habituation, beginning in childhood, in performing courageous acts. If all goes well, such a person will develop a stable psychic condition in which he can both judge well, in any given set of circumstances, the courageous thing to do and, in making that judgment, be so motivated to act. We can then say something general about courage, as Aristotle does: "The man, then, who faces and who fears the right things and with the right aim, in the right way and at the right time, and who feels confidence under the corresponding conditions, is courageous; for the courageous person feels and acts according to the merits of the case and in whatever way reason directs."[1] But there is no way to cash out "the right way," as "reason directs," other than by consulting the courageous person. The courageous thing to do can only be truly understood only from inside the courageous perspective.

Now there are two features of an ethical virtue, like courage, which are inherently linked, though they seem to tilt in opposite directions. Every ethical virtue is a source of creativity and an occasion for repetition. First, creativity: no matter how varied experience is, no matter what strange peculiarities a person may be faced with, the courageous person will be sensitive to what in those circumstances is the courageous thing to do. This requires not only a remarkable ability to interpret the situation but also the ability to make a creative response. Think of wily Odysseus: there is nothing automatic about courage.

Nevertheless, courage is also a form of repetition. For a courageous person, *every* set of circumstances and *every* action are implicitly or explicitly brought back to the question: what, in this set of circumstances, is the courageous thing to do? Everything is always and everywhere evaluated from a courageous point of view. Ironically, it is precisely the creativity of courage that will create a repetition. For no matter what the circumstances, they will be both seen and responded to in terms of courage. Courage creates the conditions of what it is to go on in the same (courageous) way.

Indeed, it is courageous repetition that helps to create a stable and accurate orientation to reality. Courage helps to organize and link one's past, present, and future. In seeing things and acting from a courageous point of view, one organizes one's life along a certain dimension. One's current perception is linked to countless past experiences: the courageous past is helping to inform and influence the courageous present and a directedness toward a courageous future. Aristotle argues that there is no greater form of human stability in the face of life's changing events (though overwhelming trauma may undermine one's happiness).[2] Ethical virtues are a paradigm of what Freud called operating according to the reality principle. As we shall see, at the heart of the reality principle there is repetition. For in reality-testing, we go back, again and again, to test our beliefs, our perceptions, our assessments of what we can achieve. The ethical virtues, for Aristotle, are vibrant, sensitive, life-enhancing ways of perceiving and living in social reality, and that is why they are manifestations of happiness—even if, in their own terms, the happiness is second-rate.

Of course, as Socrates, Plato, and Aristotle pointed out, the virtues cannot really be understood or inhabited in a piecemeal way. One cannot know, say, what the courageous thing to do is unless one is also temperate. For temperance will inform what "the right way" is, what "reason directs." Therefore, one can be truly courageous only if one is, overall, an ethically virtuous person. The ethically virtuous person will therefore be a person of practical wisdom—a *phronimos*. The *phronimos* will be able to determine in any given set of circumstances what the appropriate response is. In certain situations, say, when generosity is called for, courage will not be an obvious or immediate presence. Even so, the *phronimos* will have to be evaluating every lived circumstance in terms of courage; for even if the considered response does not give salience to courage that decision must have been made from the perspective of a courageous person.

In order to grasp the repetition of the ethical virtues, it is worth comparing it to the repetition one finds in an ordinary neurosis. For there is an uncanny resemblance. I had a patient in analysis who had the "neurotic virtue"—or, as I shall call it, the *neurtue* of disappointment. That is, she lived with an unconscious core fantasy that organized the world in terms of disappointment. Every event in life was interpreted in such a way that she was somehow being let down. The significant people in her life didn't *really* love her; they lacked the interest, the resources, or the sensitivity to give her what she really needed. In every promotion at work, the boss didn't *really* value or understand her; he was just doing it to avoid the embarrassment of leaving her alone without a raise; on every date, her partner didn't really like her, but was just trying to find something to do on a Saturday night . . . and so on.

In fact, although everything was brought back to disappointment, the person exercised creativity in making sure that this was so. Not only was she adept at interpretation—turning what, on the surface, looked like significant social and professional accomplishments, into defeats; she was also talented at acting in ways that would ensure a disappointing outcome. She implicitly or unconsciously grasped how to interact with others in ways that would provoke them to let her down. And in some strange way, she found such disappointments satisfying. There was something comforting and pleasurable about having her core fantasy—her unconscious worldview—reinforced. Neurtue is its own reward.

What, then, is the difference between neurtue and virtue? Psychoanalytic theorists tend to say that neurotic repetitions are "rigid" and "automatic"—and whatever this means precisely, I do not think it necessarily true. Certainly, some neuroses seem very constrained in the repertoire of responses, but there are so-called high-functioning neurotics who seem remarkably creative in turning the world into a disappointing place. There are, I think, three important differences. First, neurotic repetitions tend to be unconscious. From a psychoanalytic point of view, all acts will have an unconscious dimension, but at least with a virtuous act one is in a position to grasp the repetitive nature of the act. A courageous person can easily recognize his act as courageous. Second, neurotic repetitions are in some important sense unresponsive to the world.

A virtue is capacity to perceive and respond to reality in an appropriate way; a neurtue necessarily distorts reality in some way. Third, a virtuous act, at least as Aristotle understands it, is a manifestation of some form of happiness, while a neurotic response is not. There is obviously much to be said about these differences, but in terms of our current concerns, a virtue and a neurtue are identical in bringing back every action to a repetition. A courageous person frames every action in a courageous way; a neurotically disappointed person frames every act in a disappointed way.

It is precisely Freud's return to repetition that leads him to recognize a gap in psychoanalytic theory. One of the important differences between Freud and Aristotle is that Freud thought one could learn about normal functioning by examining pathological cases. And, indeed, he tended to think that extreme pathology—florid psychosis, for example—shed light on more ordinary forms of neurosis. In *Beyond the Pleasure Principle,* Freud thinks himself to the outer limits of repetition. The devastation of World War I woke him up to a peculiar type of devastation the mind can inflict on itself. "Dreams occurring in traumatic neuroses have the characteristic of repeatedly bringing the patient back to the situation of his accident, a situation from which he wakes up in another fright. *This astonishes people far too little.*"[3] What was astonishing to Freud was that there seemed to be no way to account for these dreams as disguised wish fulfillments, no way to account for them in terms of the devious functionings of the pleasure principle, for there was no way to interpret them as bearing any kind of pleasure, however hidden or conflicted.

Today we see the clinical phenomena Freud was talking about in acute cases of post-traumatic stress disorder (PTSD), so-called Vietnam War disease. I had a patient at the veterans' hospital in West Haven, Connecticut, who incessantly returned to the scene of a war atrocity. At night he would rush out of his suburban home screaming, overwhelmed with terror. He was *there,* in the war again; and occasionally he would start shooting up the suburban woods. The neighbors would then call the police and they would come, disarm him (not an easy task), and take him to the hospital. I mention this example, because it does look as though the repetition is driven in a way different from ordinary neurotic repetitions. For the latter, Freud was a master at locating hidden pleasures—unconscious to the person—that those repetitions expressed. Thus, until the traumatic neuroses of war, he could explain neurotic repetition in terms of the conflict between the pleasure principle and the reality principle (which itself is just an extension of the pleasure principle). But with the dreams of traumatic neurosis, Freud reached his limit: "We come now to a new and remarkable fact, namely that *the compulsion to repeat also recalls from the past experiences which include no possibility of pleasure,* which can never, even long ago, have brought satisfaction even to instinctual impulses which have since been repressed."[4]

I do not intend here to spell out Freud's theory of mental functioning in detail. But in order to understand Freud's conception of trauma, and why the response to it lies beyond the pleasure principle, a sketch is in order.[5] Freud isn't trying to give a detailed account of all mental and brain functioning. Rather, he is trying to work out an idealized schema of the workings of the human mind which tries to account for certain important features: namely, that it is the mind of an organism in an environment, capable of perception, thinking, and action, but also a mind which dreams, forms neurotic symptoms, and is susceptible to trauma. (He is clear that he was working with clinical psychoanalytic data and thus that he can hypothesize a mechanism based only on psychical functions and malfunctions. The hope was that future neurological research would show how this schema was actually instantiated.)

The organism has, of course, a perceptual capacity for receiving stimuli from the external world. Freud postulates that the apparatus has a certain "crust," which serves as a "protective shield," protecting the organism from being overwhelmed by stimuli from the environment. The mental mechanism itself is basically made up of neural networks of various sorts. The function of these networks is to discharge or diffuse stimuli. Each individual "neurone" is capable of receiving and storing energy, though its basic tendency is toward discharge. However, each neurone has a "contact barrier" that allows for a certain inhibition in discharge. One set of neural networks allows for a fairly free flow of energy through the system. This accounts for the loose association of ideas one finds in the construction of dreams and in neurotic symptoms. Here the energy is moving fairly quickly toward discharge in a hallucination, a dream, or a symptom. Even in this case, though, there are associations among "neurones"—neural networks—that serve to contain, diffuse, and direct the mental energy even as it moves toward discharge. But the energy in this system is fairly "mobile," and its flow through the neuronic pathways tends to dominate the system. A second, much more complex, neural network accounts for the tighter, more logical connections that one finds in reality-based conscious thinking. For this reality-based thinking to succeed, it is necessary that it further contain the free flow of energy. The mind does this by forming complex connections among "neurones" which not only connect ideas in complicated connections but also, from an economic point of view, tend to diffuse energy across the system. The energy becomes "bound" in the system. Thus thinking directed toward reality-based action—real-life satisfaction of needs and desires—can occur.

I have so far said nothing about repression or the nature of hallucination and fantasy. The important points for the moment are, first, that the mind is to a significant extent an apparatus for diffusing or discharging energy. The pleasure principle equates an increase in tension within the system with pain, a decrease with pleasure; and thus the point of mental functioning according to the pleasure principle is to decrease tension. Energy is diffused throughout a neural network—the more complex the network, the more the inhibitions of the "contact barriers"—the more the energy is both diffused and contained, even though the overall tendency of the system is toward discharge.

Second, the mind is always and everywhere working under tension. It receives stimuli from the environment and from psychosomatic sources originating in the body—and its function is to process, contain, and discharge that energy. But if an increase in tension is just what pain is, the mind is always and everywhere working in pain. Or, more accurately, the life of the mind is the metabolization of that which would, if left unmetabolized, be pain. The life of the mind is always trying to keep pain at the door.[6]

Third, at this level of generality, the difference between the mind functioning at the level of the pleasure principle and at the level of the reality principle is minimal. In both cases the mind is working toward discharge of energy; though in the latter case the route toward discharge is more circuitous, and it leads, when successful, to a real-life discharge. If all neurotic conflicts, symptoms, and other pathological phenomena could be understood in terms of conflicts between these two systems, the mind as a whole would be working *within* the pleasure principle, broadly construed.

Traumatic neurosis delivers a traumatic blow not merely to the mind, but to Freud's theory of the mind. A trauma occurs when the external stimuli are so overwhelming that they simply break through the protective shield and flood the mind:

> the pleasure principle is for the moment put out of action. There is no longer any possibility of preventing the mental apparatus from being flooded with large amounts of stimulus, and another problem arises instead—the problem of mastering the amounts of stimulus which have broken in and of binding them, in the psychical sense, so that they can be disposed of.[7]

Trauma can occur both because of overwhelming stimulation and because it itself is unprepared. Freud distinguishes anxiety from fear and fright. Anxiety is a general preparedness for an unnamed threat; fear is that preparedness directed to a particular object or situation. "Fright" is the shock and terror of being overwhelmed by surprise. The shock of trauma *to Freud's own thinking* is that he comes to realize that the pleasure principle and its variant the reality principle describe the mind only in, as it were, its *normal* pathological functioning. In traumatic neurosis Freud sees that there are more serious pathologies that attack the mind directly. And he realizes that the mind's attempt to heal itself—to restore functioning according to the pleasure principle—cannot itself be described in terms of the pleasure principle.

> The fulfilment of wishes is, as we know, brought about in a hallucinatory manner by dreams, and under the dominance of the pleasure principle this has become their function. But it is not in the service of that principle that the dreams of patients suffering from traumatic neuroses lead them back with such regularity to the situation in which the trauma occurred. We may assume, rather, that dreams are here helping to carry out another task, which must be accomplished before the dominance of the pleasure principle can even begin. *These dreams are endeavoring to master the stimulus retrospectively, by developing the anxiety whose omission was the cause of the traumatic neurosis.* They thus afford us a view of a function of the mental apparatus which, though it does not contradict the pleasure principle, is nevertheless independent of it and seems to be more primitive than the purpose of gaining pleasure and avoiding unpleasure.[8]

Freud sees the repetitive dreams of traumatic neurosis as repetitively failed attempts to install the capacity to dream (in an or-

dinary wish-fulfilling way). Anxiety, at this point in Freud's thinking, is a valuable psychological condition: it is the general state of
preparedness to deal with incoming stimulation without becoming overwhelmed. Anxiety keeps an organism ready to dream or
to think—and thus, in one way or another, to diffuse energy along
familiar neural paths. In this sense, anxiety is an important condition of mindedness—a kind of readiness for mental activity. The
impairment of the capacity to experience anxiety is thus a fundamental impairment of mind. Installing the capacity to dream turns
out to be just what it is to be ready to deal with stimuli in an anxious way.

It is ironic that it took such a destructive phenomenon as traumatic neurosis for Freud to recognize that he had overlooked the
most creative capacity of mind: the capacity to create a field of
mental functioning. Once the mind is, as it were, up and running,
it can be described as functioning according to the pleasure principle. But the pleasure principle cannot itself explain how the
conditions for its own functioning are created. Freud came relatively late to the realization that the psyche itself is a psychological
achievement —the idea is first expressed in his 1914 essay "The
Introduction of Narcissism." The 1920 recognition that there
must be activities of mind that function beyond the pleasure principle is, really, a continuation of that insight.

> This would seem to be the place, then, to admit for the
> first time an exception to the proposition that dreams are
> fulfilments of wishes . . . it is impossible to classify as
> wish-fulfilments the dreams we have been discussing

which occur in traumatic neuroses, or the dreams during psychoanalysis which bring to memory the psychical traumas of childhood. They arise, rather, in *obedience to the compulsion to repeat,* though it is true that in analysis the compulsion is supported by the wish (which is encouraged by "suggestion") to conjure up what has been forgotten and repressed. Thus it would seem that the function of dreams, which consists in setting aside any motives that might interrupt sleep, by fulfilling the wishes of the disturbing impulses, *is not their original function.* It would not be possible for them to perform that function until the whole of mental life had accepted the dominance of the pleasure principle. If there is a "beyond the pleasure principle" it is only consistent to grant that *there was also a time before the purpose of dreams was the fulfilment of wishes.* This would imply no denial of their later function.[9]

The significance, then, of the traumatic neurosis is that it enables Freud to isolate a fundamental mental force—the compulsion to repeat—which functions *before* the pleasure principle. And it is because this force continues to function even after the pleasure principle is established that Freud can talk of a "beyond": "we shall find courage to assume that there really does exist in the mind a compulsion to repeat which overrides the pleasure principle."[10]

But once Freud finds the compulsion to repeat in this pure form, he is then able to find instances of it virtually everywhere. As he says at the close of his essay, "many processes take place in mental life independently of the pleasure principle."[11] In particular, the repetitions and actings out which occur in the analysis of the transference neuroses are no longer to be conceptualized in terms of the unconscious functionings of the pleasure principle gaining some (disguised) expression, but rather as breakings through of the compulsion to repeat. Freud's point is that early psychosocial development is inherently so traumatic—so marked by unpreparedness, by blows to a fragile ego, by tragic reversal and loss—that the repetitions that occur within psychoanalytic treatment should be regarded as mini-explosions of the compulsion to repeat. They are similar in form to the explosions of the traumatic neuroses, if less intense.

Patients repeat all of these unwanted situations and painful emotions in the transference and revive them with the greatest ingenuity. They seek to bring about the interruption of the treatment while it is still incomplete; they contrive once more to feel themselves scorned, to oblige the physician to speak severely to them and treat them coldly; they discover appropriate objects for their jealousy; instead of the passionately desired baby of their childhood, they produce a plan or a promise of some grand present—that turns out as a rule to be no less unreal. None of these things can have produced pleasure in the past, and it might be supposed that they would cause less unpleasure today if they emerged as memories or dreams instead of taking the form of fresh experiences. They are of course the activities of instincts intended to lead to satisfaction; but no lesson has been learnt from the old experience of these activities having led instead only to unpleasure. In spite of that, *they are repeated, under pressure of a compulsion.*[12]

One can now see why Freud said that the repetitions of the repetition compulsion have astonished people too little. In effect, Freud is here admitting that his entire theory of the transference neuroses, his theory of psychoanalytic therapy and cure, needs to be revised. And it has to be revised to account for a fundamental mental force that Freud admits he doesn't really understand.

> But if a compulsion to repeat does operate in the mind, we should be glad to know something about it, to learn what function it corresponds to, under what conditions it can emerge and what its relation is to the pleasure principle—to which, after all, we have hitherto ascribed dominance over the course of the processes of excitation in mental life.[13]

At this point, all that Freud knows is that the "compulsion to repeat" functions differently from the one principle of mental functioning he really does understand, the pleasure principle.

It seems to me difficult to overestimate the importance of Freud's theoretical next step for the future of psychoanalysis. For if the repetitions of the transference neuroses—that is, the repetitions that occur within the context of psychoanalytic treatment— are manifestations of the compulsion to repeat, we really don't know what they are or what we, as analysts, are doing with them until we understand this compulsion. This is nothing less than a revolutionary moment in the history of psychoanalysis. And it is a moment in which Freud takes a series of crucial missteps.

Why, after all, consider the compulsion to repeat a compulsion *to* repeat? If we stick close to the clinical data of the traumatic neuroses, all we know is that they do have a compulsive power and that they issue in repetitions. But to talk of a compulsion *to* repeat is to suggest that the aim or the point of the compulsion is to produce a repetition—that is, it is implicitly to import a teleological assumption about the functioning of the compulsion. And for this, as yet, we have no evidence.

On the contrary, there is a more austere hypothesis that better fits the evidence: that the mind has a tendency to disrupt itself, that these disruptions are not *for* anything—they are devoid of purpose. Indeed, insofar as mind is teleologically organized, these disruptions disrupt teleology. What appears as a repetition occurs, as it were, later, in the mind's attempt to form a defense against disruption. Indeed, Freud's own clinical observations point in this direction. As Freud himself says: in traumatic dreams the mind is "endeavoring to master the stimulus *retrospectively*."[14] The "compulsion to repeat" would not in this case be a basic psychological phenomenon, in need of an explanation of its aim, but would rather be the epiphenomenal manifestation of the *failure* of a defense. Because the veteran cannot dream he is repetitively brought back to the scene of the atrocity. But that is not because there is some elemental insistence that this scene be repeated, but because the mental efforts to lend meaning to a meaningless disruption—an external trauma or internal self-disruption—abort.

Freud, as we have seen, says: "Dreams occurring in traumatic neuroses have the characteristic of repeatedly bringing the patient back to the situation of his accident, a situation from which he wakes up in another fright. This astonishes people far too little." It now appears that he was astonished by the wrong thing. Freud seems to think that what is astonishing is that the patient is repetitively brought back to "the situation of his accident," whereas what is astonishing is that "he wakes up in another fright." That is, what is astonishing is that once the mind has been traumatized (by a real-life event), it will begin to traumatize itself. It will continue to induce its own "fright" or shock—and this self-disruption cannot be occurring according to the pleasure principle. That the patient is repeatedly brought back to the situation is a defensive response to self-disruption. It is the stillborn attempt to heal the wound by dreaming a meaning. There would be no appearance of repetition if this attempt to supply content to experience fully succeeded. The mind would simply move on—going down myriad paths of connected meanings. What we see as a "repetition" is a partial success—the beginnings of content—and partial failure—the inability to knit this hanging thread into the fabric of experience.

Conversely, if the patient manifested only contentless anxiety attacks, he would be diagnosed as having a panic disorder or as suffering anxiety. Even if the anxiety attacks happened over and over, there would be no interest in the repetition *as such:* our practical and theoretical interest would focus on the anxiety. It is the content of the traumatic dream (or symptomatic act) that brings the idea of repetition to the fore.

Here a comparison with Darwin's theory of natural selection is in order. To put it in the terms of the current discussion, Darwin argued that living nature had an inherent tendency to disrupt itself.[15] That is, random mutations would occur within the reproductive cells of living organisms which would, in effect, allow nature to "try out" new combinations. If the new organism could survive in the environment long enough to reproduce, so be it. It would then look as though this creature was designed to live in this environment. But the appearance of design was illusory; what Darwin explained was the functioning of *as-if* teleology. Of course, within this overall context, there may be strivings of various sorts. Creatures in an environment will be striving to reproduce. It is not, then, that all purpose is lacking. Darwin's point is that the self-disruptions of nature are not themselves the expression of a purpose nor is nature the product of a grand design.

Now suppose there were certain attempts at sexual reproduction that tended to abort. Apparently, it is the case that in certain polluted lakes in the United States, frogs will interact with some of the pollutants in a way that regularly produces the same sort of monstrosity: a certain kind of deformed frog embryo or tadpole that will die before it can reproduce. The environment, one might say, delivers a trauma to the organism. And frogs respond by producing the same kind of monstrosity over and over again. No one would in this case think that there is here manifested a "compulsion to repeat." Rather, one would think that there are certain kinds of disruptions which nature cannot "heal over" with a successful mutation.

Of course, there is a certain kind of striving to be found in this situation: frogs are striving to reproduce.[16] And if they had suc-ceeded in reproducing offspring that could reproduce, the frogs would, in effect, have healed over a wound delivered by the envi-ronment. But the fact that frog efforts at reproduction fail—that monstrosities and miscarriages emerge—reveals nothing more than a traumatic breakdown in the goal-directed activity of sexual reproduction. To attribute a teleological purpose to the break-down itself—as though it were manifesting a "compulsion to re-peat"—would be to misconstrue what is happening. This seems to me to be a rare instance in which Freud's overall strategy of using pathological cases to shed light on mindedness in general comes to grief. For what we are looking at here is, I think, a misfire—an aborted attempt at mindedness—not, as Freud thinks, a directed movement of the mind.

The insight that Freud opened up but could not really grasp is that some mental activity occurs without a purpose. Freud cannot see this because all of this thinking and research is directed toward finding hidden and deeper purposes. Freud uses the phenomenon of the "repetition compulsion" to speculate about the ultimate purpose of the drives:

> But how is the predicate of being "driven" related to the compulsion to repeat? At this point we cannot escape a suspicion that we may have come upon the track of a universal attribute of drives and perhaps of organic life in general which has not hitherto been clearly recognized or at least not explicitly stressed. *It seems, then, that a drive is an urge inherent in organic life to restore an earlier state of*

things which the living entity has been obliged to abandon, under the pressure of external disturbing forces . . .

This view of drives strikes us as strange because we have become used to see in them a factor impelling towards change and development, whereas we are now asked to recognize in them the precise contrary—an expression of the *conservative* nature of living substance.[17]

If one does not emphasize the repetition, there is no basis for conceptualizing the drive as aimed at the restoration of an earlier state of things. And if there is no basis for seeing the drives as inherently tending toward "the same thing again," then there is no basis for conceiving the drives as essentially conservative. If, by contrast, one sees the mind as inherently self-disruptive, there is no need to see those disruptions as moving in any direction at all. Rather, they provide occasions on which the mind *may* respond by taking up one direction or another. Freud misunderstands the nature of the drive not only because he is searching for hidden purpose, but because he misunderstands what is being repeated. The "repetition" is not of content, but of activity—the activity of self-disruption. Such disruptiveness in no way "tends" toward restoration—it "tends" just as much toward the new mental creations. In fact it tends in no direction at all.[18]

Freud moves from the idea that the compulsion to repeat is fundamental and not in the service of the pleasure principle to the idea that the fundamental nature of the drives is to restore an earlier state of things—and from there he moves on to the so-called death drive.

For the moment it is tempting to pursue to its logical conclusion the hypothesis that all drives tend towards the restoration of an earlier state of things . . .

Let us suppose, then, that all organic drives are conservative, are acquired historically and tend towards the restoration of an earlier state of things. It follows that the phenomena of organic development must be attributed to external disturbing or diverting influences. The elementary living entity would from its very beginning have had no wish to change; if conditions remained the same, it would do no more than constantly repeat the same course of life. In the last resort, what has left its mark on the development of organisms must be the history of the earth we live in and of its relation to the sun. Every modification which is thus imposed upon the course of the organism's life is accepted by the conservative organic drives and stored up for further repetition. Those drives are therefore bound to give a deceptive appearance of being forces tending toward change and progress, whilst in fact they are merely seeking to reach an ancient goal by paths alike old and new. Moreover, *it is possible to specify this final goal of all organic striving*. It would be in contradiction to the conservative nature of the drives if the goal of life were a state of things which had never been attained. On the contrary, it must be an old state of things, an initial state from which the living entity has at one time or another departed and to which it is striving to return by the circuitous paths along which its developments leads. If we are to take it as a truth that knows no exception that everything living dies for internal reasons—becomes inorganic once again—then we shall be compelled to say that *"the aim of all life is death"* . . .[19]

Freud has made his career by finding hidden meanings—regularly tending in directions opposite to the conscious purposes and intentions of his patients. What greater accomplishment than to uncover the hidden meaning of all life—and to discover that it is really moving in the opposite direction to its appearance of life-filled striving?[20] In effect, Freud is attempting to substitute one form of teleological striving for another. Before Freud—as Freud understands it—the preponderant theoretical tendency was to see living organisms as each striving toward its own good. Whether one appealed to Aristotelian forms or to Darwinian natural selection, organisms were seen as having innate developmental tendencies pushing them in the direction of healthy growth, maturation, and flourishing. Freud's attempted reversal here is to insist that all this is only the *manifest content* of life. When we meditate on the compulsion to repeat, we can think through this appearance to a deeper level and see that, really, "the aim of all life is death."

Obviously, what I am suggesting is that Freud should have used his insight not to offer a reverse and hidden teleology but, in this instance, to abandon the appeal to a teleological principle. The point of the mind's self-disruptions is, well . . . nothing at all.

Now this does not mean there cannot be motivated repetitions. Of course there can. The only point is that there is no evidence to suggest that the repetitions emerge from a fundamental force for repetition. Again a comparison with Darwin is apt: a change in an organism that emerges more or less randomly may acquire a function and subsequently get selected for. In a similar way, a person who gets stuck in a particular way may come to fixate on that form of stuckness. I had a patient who on one occasion had difficulty closing the outer door to my office as he entered. The door is somewhat difficult to close—it is a heavy outer door, on slow hinges, with an old-fashioned latch. On the first occasion he tried for a bit, then gave up in embarrassment. However, subsequently not closing the door became a symptom. Having emerged in life, it was over time invested with a wealth of different meanings: that he could escape the analysis, that I should help him, that nothing he was going to say was so important it could not be overheard, that he was leaving his mind open, that someone should come in and watch us, and so on. Obviously, not closing the door became a motivated repetition. But this is not because there is a fundamental force in the mind for repetition, but because a relatively idiosyncratic event became a vehicle for expressing all sorts of idiosyncratic meanings. Something ends up becoming a repetition because of what happens next.

In my reading, Freud introduces "death" in much the same way that Aristotle introduces "*the* good": as an enigmatic signifier that is supposed to give us the goal of *all* striving. Really, we have no better understanding of what Freud means by "death" than we do of what Aristotle means by "*the* good." Each is injected into our thought in the hope of allowing us to organize our experience in such a way as to see all striving as directed toward *that*. But there is no real content to *that*. In this way, Freud attempts a seduction in very much the same sense that Aristotle does. He injects an enigmatic signifier into our thinking, a signifier around which circulate in his own mind profound unconscious meanings. And he puts it forward as an explanatory end-of-the-line. And it is here that Freud misses the significance of his own insight: what lies "beyond the pleasure principle" isn't another principle, but a lack of principle.

I do not mean to dismiss Freud's act. Freud is, I think, opening up a new field of possibilities for human self-understanding. What he reveals is a structural truth about mindedness in general: that mind by its very nature works under conditions of pressure and that there is an overall tendency in the system toward discharge. This insight opens up new possibilities for thinking about creativity and destructiveness in the mind.[21] But by naming this tendency "death," Freud seduces himself into thinking that he has discovered a principle within the system —a certain sort of "thing." This is an ontological mistake. He thinks he has discovered a something when what he has recognized is not another thing, but a truth about the way the mind works (as Heidegger would put it, a truth about the being of the mind).

In effect, Freud is enacting the traumatic theory in his own construction of a theory of trauma. The fact that the mind disrupts itself in ways that simply do not fit the functionings of the pleasure principle disrupts Freud's own thinking. It provokes, as it were, a trauma in psychoanalytic theory. Freud tries to contain this disruption—and give it a meaning—by calling it "death." But in so doing, he covers over the disruption. What, on the surface, looks as though it is an answer to the question of what is happening here is in fact a covering over of the question with the appearance of an enigmatic "answer."

The result is of significance for psychoanalysis. Freud tries to use the death drive to bring under one concept what, on the surface, look like three different types of phenomena. First, there is the structural idea that the mind works under tension and tends toward discharge. Freud's model of the mind since the *Project* has been one of the mind's working to diffuse and discharge energy. At first it may look as though the mind tends toward homeostasis: trying to maintain a constant level of energy. But Freud's point is that if one looks at the model broadly enough one will see that the functioning of the pleasure principle is simply *toward discharge*. The relatively temporary maintenance of homeostasis can then be viewed as a temporary detour of life *en route* to death. In this sense, the pleasure principle can be seen as, overall, working in the service of the death drive. As Freud says, "The pleasure principle seems actually to serve the death instincts."[22] (By way of analogy: the healthy human organism tends to maintain a temperature of 98.6°F. In day-to-day healthy living we may not notice that any effort is involved, but we certainly notice when the organism stops making this effort, for then it assumes room temperature.)

Second, there is the idea that repetition is the aim of all drives, and that that should be understood as the attempt to restore an earlier state of things. Here Freud is able to introduce a teleological principle.

Third, Freud uses the death drive to account for human aggression. For Freud, the death drive is an internal tendency of the organism—a tendency manifest in every cell of the biological organism as well as a tendency internal to the mind. Aggression is that tendency *deflected outward*.[23] It is this third phenomenon, human aggression, that is, from the current point of view, of greatest significance. In *Civilization and Its Discontents,* Freud admits astonishment that he so long "overlooked the ubiquity of non-erotic aggressivity and destructiveness and can have failed to give it its due place in our interpretation of life."[24] That is, *in retrospect*—from what he takes to be the safe vantage of one who now has a theory of aggression—Freud can recognize that he had, previous to invention of the theory, overlooked or deflected the problem of nonerotic aggression. In this way, the theory of the death drive fills in what would otherwise be a significant gap in psychoanalytic theory. But if what I have been saying is correct, the "theory of the death drive" is a theory in name only. In fact, it doesn't fill in any gap; it couldn't, because it is the injection of an enigmatic signifier. What it covers over is the fact that psychoanalysis lacks a theory of aggression.

This claim, of course, needs explanation and qualification. From Melanie Klein and her followers we have learned much about the content and vicissitudes of certain aggressive fantasies, especially those which occur in the paranoid-schizoid position. Indeed, we do have a valuable theory of certain paradigmatic defenses: the paranoid-schizoid and depressive positions. From Wilfrid Bion we have learned how the mind can attack its own functioning; from D. W. Winnicott we have learned much about infantile rage and the rage of the analyst; from Paul Gray we have learned how an aggressive superego can attack even the microstructure of sentence formation; and so on.[25] There is, then, no shortage of valuable psychoanalytic discussions of aggression. But important as these discussions are, theoretically speaking they all stand at about the same level as Freud's discussion of the oedipus complex in his account of human sexuality. No doubt, the oedipus complex is a fundamental structure for our understanding of the fate of human sexuality, but it is not itself a theory of sexuality. For that, Freud gives us a detailed account of the sexual drive. In the *Three Essays on the Theory of Sexuality* and in *The Interpretation of Dreams,* Freud gives us a detailed account of how the sexual drive works: a theory of "propping," of primary-process mental functioning, of hallucinatory gratification, fantasy, and symptom formation. We are then in a position to see, for example, the oedipus complex as arising out of the vicissitudes of the sexual drive. There is no equivalent account of the "aggressive drive": so far, it is only a place-holder for that, whatever it is, which causes these manifestations of aggression.

The theory of the death drive makes it *look* as though it is offering a real theory—linking aggression up to other phenomena and forces—but it is only a seductive gesture in the direction of a theory. I regularly hear psychoanalytic thinkers say that such-and-such an aggressive fantasy is "a manifestation of the death drive" or "a manifestation of the aggressive drive"—without realizing that this additional term adds nothing to what they have already said. For these phrases to add content we would need already to have a worked-out theory of the death drive or aggressive drive—and this, so far, we lack. Simply injecting an enigmatic signifier is not enough.

That is why the bringing together of the tendency toward discharge, the repetition compulsion, and aggression under the "concept" of Death is a seduction: for it *looks* as though Freud is pulling off a theoretical unification and simplification. And it *looks* as though he is reaching ultimate principles—an explanatory Archimedean point. What he is in fact doing is injecting an oracular utterance into psychoanalysis: something that *looks* as though it is revealing a deep and hidden meaning about us, but whose content will depend on what we do with it.

I am not attacking the very idea of a psychoanalytic theory of aggression, but opening up the possibility of forming one. To do this, we need to recognize that we don't yet have a theory, just a fantasy of having one. There is an important structural truth that Freud has uncovered: that the mind works under conditions of tension and tends toward discharge. But this should not be confused with a metaphysical principle. We can avoid this confusion if we refuse to take Freud's first step. Instead of viewing the outbursts of traumatic neurosis as a pure instance of an elemental force—the repetition compulsion—we should see it as a dramatic instance of mental self-disruption that is met with repetitively failing attempts to lend meaning.[26] The mind's tendency to disrupt itself is not itself good or bad; indeed, it is not a principle of any teleological system. It exists *before good and evil*. Whether what follows is good or bad depends upon what happens next—and upon the individual's entire previous history of happenings next. In other words, instead of seeing this disruptive tendency as either an "aggressive" drive or as a force for unification, one should see it as prior to both, but as providing an occasion for either.

Consider Freud's account of a child's invention of a game:

> Theories [of children's play] attempt to discover the motives which lead children to play, but they fail to bring into the foreground the *economic* motive, the consideration of the yield of pleasure involved . . . I have been able, through a chance opportunity which presented itself, to throw some light upon the first game played by a little boy of one and a half and invented by himself . . . it was some time before I discovered the meaning of this puzzling activity which he constantly repeated.
>
> The child was not at all precocious in his intellectual development . . . He was, however, on good terms with his parents and their one servant-girl, and tributes were paid to his being a "good boy." He did not disturb his parents at night, he conscientiously obeyed orders not to touch certain things or go into certain rooms, and *above all he never cried when his mother left him for a few hours.* At the same time, he was greatly attached to his mother, who had not only fed him herself but had also looked after him without any outside help. This good little boy, however, had an occasional *disturbing habit* of taking any small objects he could get hold of and throwing them away from him into a corner under a bed, and so on, so that hunting for his toys and picking them up was often quite a business. As he did this he gave vent to a loud, long-drawn-out

"o-o-o-o," accompanied by an expression of interest and satisfaction. His mother and the writer of this present account were agreed in thinking that this was not a *mere interjection* but represented the German word *"fort"* [gone]. I eventually realized that it was a game and that the only use he made of any of his toys was to play "gone" with them. One day I made an observation which confirmed my view. The child had a wooden reel with a piece of string tied round it. It never occurred to him to pull it along the floor behind him, for instance, and play at its being a carriage. What he did was to hold the reel by the string and very skillfully throw it over the edge of his curtained cot, so that it disappeared into it, at the same time uttering his expressive "o-o-o-o." He then pulled the reel out of the cot again by the string and hailed its reappearance with a joyful *"da"* [there]. This then was the complete game— disappearance and return. *As a rule one only witnessed the first act, which was repeated untiringly as a game in itself, though there is no doubt that the greater pleasure was attached to the second act.*

The interpretation of the game then became obvious. It was related to the child's great cultural achievement— the instinctual renunciation (that is, the renunciation of instinctual satisfaction) which he had made in *allowing his mother to go away without protesting. He compensated himself for this, as it were, by himself staging the disappearance and return of the objects within his reach.* It is of course a matter of indifference from the point of view of judging the effec-

tive nature of the game whether the child invented it himself or took it over on some outside suggestion. Our interest is direct to another point. *The child cannot possibly have
felt his mother's departure as something agreeable or even indif-
ferent. How then does his repetition of this distressing experience
of a game fit in with the pleasure principle?*[27]

This is a profile in (the development of) courage. Aristotle insists
that we need to be habituated into the ethical virtues, and I think
we can here see Freud examining the prehistory of that psychic
development. The game is prompted by a rip in the fabric of life.
If we are trying to respect the child's point of view, we cannot
even say that the game is prompted by loss. For it is only after the
game is installed that the child will begin to have the concept of
loss or absence. Only when the game is established will the loss be
a loss *for him*. The outcome of the game is to convert what would
otherwise be a nameless trauma into a loss. The child had been inhabiting a less differentiated field of "mother-and-child": it is this
field that is disturbed by the mother's absence.

Once the rip has occurred the child experiences *internal pressure* to enact the disturbance. Freud says that what is distinctive
about his theory of child's play is that he foregrounds "the economic motive." He is quite right to stress the economic aspect,
but wrong to treat economics as a motive. That is, we are concerned with psychic pressure—with the intensity of mental life—
and thus there is some sense to invoking the idea of quantities of
energy. But we speak of quantities here precisely because there is
no motive: just a buildup of pressure. And now there is an enact-

ment of self-disruption: the child throws away the spool and says "o-o-o-o." This is a moment of self-disruption in an already disrupted life. What this disruption is *for* really depends on what happens next.

Let us imagine a very different outcome for this child from the one that actually occurred. Suppose the child could never get to "da." He would then get stuck repeating "o-o-o-o" over and over again. We would then see something that looked like a traumatic neurosis. Indeed, the child might begin to use these outbursts to attack his own mind. For the child would never be able to get a thought together if each attempt to do so was interrupted by an outburst of "o-o-o-o."[28] Rather than face the loss, the child might opt to attack his own ability to understand what has happened to him. This would be the beginning of a massively self-destructive, self-annihilating character.

There is no place in Aristotle's ontology for such a character. For Aristotle, all the possibilities of human being—the virtuous person, the merely continent person, the incontinent, and the wicked person—are oriented toward the good. Even the bad person is oriented toward what he mistakenly thinks is good. The conflicted person experiences a conflict among goods, and irrationality is explained in terms of a person's opting for a good in contradiction to his conscious judgment of what is best. In the case of the self-annihilating character, by contrast, there is an attack on any attempt to orient oneself toward the good. It is an attack upon the capacity to be a teleologically directed creature—and in that sense is an attack upon the good itself. This is one reason why we cannot think of psychoanalysis as providing an occasion to expand an Aristotelian approach to ethics to include a broader range of motivation. For what we have here is not a form of motivation—it is not directed toward any good, no matter how distorted the image—but rather a primitive attack on the capacity to form motivation.

But the same disturbance can also provide an occasion for the early development of virtue. In being able to get to "da," the child is able to bring his experience together rather than blow it apart. The invention of the game converts this rip in the fabric of experience into an experience of loss. It creates a cultural space in which the child can play with loss: in this way he comes to be able to tolerate it and name it. This is an instance in which a way of functioning according to the pleasure principle and a way of functioning according to the reality principle get installed at the same time. On the one hand, all sorts of playfulness and loose associations are now possible: it is only now that the mind can wander around the idea of mother's absence. On the other hand, it is only in this play that the concept of mother's absence (and reappearance) emerges. One might say that the child has either invented or joined a form of life in which mother exists as a distinct "object"—one who can be present, go away, and come back again, all the while maintaining (what now emerges as) her distinct identity. Inventing the game, the child thereby creates the capacity *to think* about mother's absence. It is precisely in the creation of these sorts of playful activities that a child enters the space of reasons.

This is courage-in-the-making. For it requires that the child tolerate mother's absence. And the game actually is the development of protocourage; for he endures mother's actual absence by playing with it. He thus imagines her (as absent, as present) in her absence, and thus develops the capacity to tolerate her absence by reassuring himself imaginatively that she will return. This is the paradigm of the idea that it takes courage to face reality. In this sense, courage (or this prototype) seems to be a necessary constituent of mindedness itself. For we can think, in any realistic sense, only when we can think about absent objects. To be able to do this requires the emotional ability to tolerate absence. In this first instance, courage is directed not toward happiness, but away from pain. One relieves pain by giving it a name, but to name the experience is to transform it. The child has, in effect, spontaneously injected a name into his own life. But there is no such thing as just "introducing a name." The name of loss requires the game of loss: it requires inventing ways of living with the loss that one has just named. Once the game is established, once the child can face his loss courageously, once the mind can function according to the pleasure principle, the question of what lies beyond (or before) gets covered over. What gets hidden is the nonteleological occasion for courage: the disruption of the fabric of life to which courage can be only a retrospective response. Once the child can experience the loss as a loss—that is, once the child has established the game—he is no longer experiencing that which was the occasion for the development of the capacity to experience loss. If we think of a name as standing unproblematically for that which it names, then an *inaugural* act of naming like this always misses its mark. In this sense, "facing reality" always leaves something out. The child can now experience his loss, name his loss, and react to

it—he is emotionally and cognitively "in touch with reality"—
and thus it looks as though nothing could possibly be left out. He
is living, so it appears, *without remainder*. What does get left out,
to put it paradoxically, is not another "thing," but a disturbance of
the fabric of life which occasioned this further development of the
capacity to face reality. Freud's deepest insight, I suspect, is that,
appearances to the contrary, life can never be lived without
remainder.

It is worth noting how the invention of this game fits Freud's
model of mental functioning. In effect, the invention of the game
serves to establish a homeostatic mechanism in the child's mind.
The psychic pressure that builds up as a result of mother's absence—or, now, to any buildup of tension—is diffused along
connecting paths of neural networks. From the perspective of
subjective experience, this is a movement of energy along a loose
association of ideas and feelings that lend meaning to the disturbance. The child is, as it were, pressured into creating meaning.
Without the game, the pressure would just break through and the
child would be overcome with fright or flooded with anxiety. The
game is that which enables the child to keep his emotional and
mental balance. And it is reasonable to assume that the establishment of this homeostatic system facilitates further such development. The child not only learns to tolerate his mother's absence;
he learns that he *can* so tolerate her absence. Thus there forms a
disposition to create such homeostatic systems through imaginative activity. This is an essential stage in the laying down of courage as a psychic disposition.

This is a major psychic accomplishment, but the child did not do it all on his own. He is born into a social world of parents and extended family that is listening to (and interpreting) his every "o-o-o-o." Freud reports that he and the child's mother "were agreed in thinking that this was not a *mere interjection* but represented the German word *'fort.'*" As I understand the situation, the outburst *became* more than a mere interjection, in part because it was treated as being more than one. In effect, Freud and the mother offer the child an interpretation of his outburst: and thus they help him convert his "disturbing habit" into a game of loss. From this perspective, it is not just that "o-o-o-o" sounds like *fort*, but that *fort* sounds like "o-o-o-o." It is that resemblance which helps the parents and family draw the child further into the social and meaningful world.

There is, then, a nest of constituent moments in the construction of the child's game: (1) the development of the capacity to play: the ability to let the mind slip along paths of loose associations— from mother to spool, from gone to here. From the point of view of the mental apparatus, this is what it is (2) to establish a series of neural "facilitations"—neural pathways—along which energy can flow and be diffused according to the pleasure principle. At the same time this is (3) the development of the reality principle: the development of the capacity to recognize that mother is a distinct "object" from "me," one who has gone away, but who will return.[29] This is what it is (4) to enter the space of reasons: the child is developing the capacity to think about mother's absence and to think about what he wants to do about that. It is also (5) the development of courage: the ability to face and tolerate a primal loss. In this sense, (6) the installation of a homeostatic mechanism, along the lines of Freud's model, is equivalent to Aristotle's conception of ethical virtue as striking "the mean" between too much and too little. Moreover, (7) the child is being inducted into the ethical and linguistic world by parents and family who help to lend meaning to his utterances. Finally, if we take all of these moments into consideration, they suggest (8) the emergence of a teleologically organized agent. This is a person who can create fantasies directed toward imagined goods, who can think about his real good and act on it, who can exercise courage and thereby orient his life toward happiness. We see here the birth of teleology in an agent. These constituent moments are not acquired piecemeal; all emerge together in the creation of this game.

By now it should be clear that there are certain structural similarities between Aristotle's treatment of happiness and Freud's treatment of death. Happiness and death are each invoked as the purported aim of all striving. Aristotle and Freud's project is to grasp the totality—to say what all human striving is a striving toward. The assumption is that nothing gets left out, that a teleological organized system will explain what is important about human existence. Now each thinker, in the very activity of describing human directedness, realizes that there is something important *outside* of that directedness. But he tries to capture that outside in teleological terms. Aristotle begins by setting happiness as a constituent end of ethical life, but he concludes that the deepest understanding of ethical life must see it as pointing beyond itself. Thus he is led to formulate two grades of happiness: the second-rate happiness of the ethical life, and the first-rate happiness of the life that is oriented toward contemplation. It is important for Aristotle that contemplation is a *higher* form of activity, but from our point of view the important feature is that ethical life is directed toward a form of existence that lies outside the ethical and is in itself totally impractical. Freud begins by thinking he can capture all human striving (conscious and unconscious) in terms of the pleasure principle and its variant, the reality principle. But he too comes to realize that much of human existence lies beyond (or before) such striving: in particular, the activities of installing the various capacities to be directed and primitive attacks upon those capacities. He himself tries to install the death drive as a more general principle which will both capture the strivings of the pleasure principle and give a conceptual framework in which the "beyond" of the pleasure principle can itself be seen as a bizarre sort of striving on its own. Each in his own way sees a "beyond" of teleology; each in his own way is reluctant to leave teleology behind.

For both thinkers an ethical virtue, such as courage, emerges both as a source of happiness and pleasure and as tiring. For Freud, this is easy to see. Once the *fort-da* game, the prototype of courage, is installed it serves to discharge tension along familiar paths of associations. The discharge itself is pleasurable—the game is fun to play—and insofar as it is a courageous response to loss, Aristotle would agree that it is the stuff of which happiness is made. But the game is played under tension—indeed, it is a playing out of that tension—and insofar as one is drawn to that game over and over again, one is living in the service of diffusing tension. The impulse which creatively installs this game, or which breaks it down to make room for another, is beyond the pleasure principle. Without this "beyond," life would be repetitive and relentless. The game is fun only if we can invent it, resort to it at will, and leave it behind when we start to get sick of it. Without the ability to leave this game, we are stuck in a routine. There is something tiring about striking the mean (or, as Freud would put it, maintaining a constant level of energy). For Aristotle, it is hard to get away from the idea that courage is both a source and a manifestation of happiness. The statesman's life is the highest exemplification of the ethical virtues, and thus it is a happy life. But we have already seen Aristotle say that the statesman's life is unleisurely and points to a happiness beyond itself.[30] If one remained stuck in the courageous life of a statesman, there would be happiness, to be sure, but one would also be confined to an unleisurely life—one which was properly directed toward a happiness one would never achieve.

Both thinkers agree that there is an important "beyond" to ethical virtue, but they misconstrue that "beyond" because they themselves remain stuck in teleology. They are able to do this because they misconstrue their own theoretical activity. Each has, in effect, injected an enigmatic signifier into life and thought, but each takes himself to have discovered a fundamental goal. In this sense, Aristotle and Freud seduce themselves. What would have taken them to a real understanding of their "beyonds" would have been a proper understanding of their own activity. For precisely by installing an enigmatic signifier—whether happiness or death—Aristotle and Freud break up old and established lines of thought and provide occasion for a creative re-invention of life. It is *this* activity that lies beyond the pleasure principle, beyond the established ethical virtues. And to cultivate it is certainly not to cultivate yet another ethical virtue. What, then, is it?

Let me close here with a flight of fancy. In the *Republic,* Socrates says that the same structures that exist in the psyche can be seen writ large in the polis.[31] One can, I think, view the life of Socrates as a political enactment of the same types of movement that we have been trying to follow inside the psyche. Socrates' life is an incessant source of disruption to the established customs of Athenian life. Socrates seems to see himself in just this way, for he characterizes himself as a gadfly.[32] He is Athens' incarnation of the "repetition compulsion." He is always asking questions: What is piety? What is temperance? What is courage? And he repeatedly invites his fellow citizens to recognize that neither he nor anyone else knows the answers. This would suggest that, as yet, there *are* no answers. Socrates is trying to establish a new kind of thinking, and a life with that thinking has not yet been constituted.[33] Thus the ceaseless repetition of Socratic questioning bears a family resemblance to the repetitive dreams and acts of traumatic neurosis. The capacity to think, answer and live in a Socratic manner has not yet been established—that is ultimately why Socrates is unique[34]—but he is preparing the way for the inaugurating instantiations that Plato and Aristotle will make.

Socrates' fundamental question—how shall I live?—looks so innocent but is in fact traumatic. Socrates rips open the fabric of Athenian life and creates a gap which no one can fill, for as yet there is no established way of taking one's whole life into account in everything that one does. In Freudian terms, Socrates is an incarnation of the death drive: an aggressive puncture in the established modes of life and thought, an occasion for forming new ways of living and thinking.

The Athenians react to this trauma by trying to kill it off. The killing of Socrates manifests a psychotic understanding of how to get rid of a disruption: one treats a nonthing as though it were a thing and then destroys it.[35] On this reading, Socrates is guilty as charged. He does introduce a new god insofar as he introduces a new standard of evaluation—the "happiness" of our lives considered *as a whole*—and treats it as a fundamental measure. And he does corrupt the youth in the sense that he seduces them. Not only does he introduce an enigmatic signifier into life, around which all our speculations about living can circulate; in so doing, he drives the boys wild. One has only to observe Apollodorus, Aristodemus, Agathon, Alcibiades to see that Socrates kills them all softly, with his words.[36] Socrates *is* a traumatizing seducer: he is guilty of the repetitive introjection into life of a message that life cannot contain.

Freud's insight into the structure of society is that it is only when one kills off the messenger that the message finally gets installed. One can view Socrates as the ancient Greek, homosexual instantiation of the primal father. From the perspective of the Athenian citizens who sat on the jury, Socrates' insistence that even established custom needed reflective examination placed him outside the law. And if one substitutes intellectual prowess for overtly sexual activity, it is clear that Socrates can have *all* the boys. In response to Socrates' murder, Plato invents philosophy as an act of mourning. Indeed, the very name "philosophy" characterizes the activity as a distinctive kind of longing for the lost object. *Philosophia,* love of wisdom: the philosopher is a person who strives for something he knows he does not yet have.[37] Indeed, Platonic philosophy can be seen as a sublimated and sophisticated variant of the *fort-da* game. In the *Republic,* Plato is playing with Socrates' absence and return. A significant part of the *Republic* is given over to an account of the structure of the human psyche, one which is designed to make clear the kinds of irrational forces that could lead to the killing of a good man. And the rest is, really, Plato's *dream* of a society in which Socrates could come back and rule. The "beautiful city" (the *kallipolis*) is Plato's field of dreams: a place where philosophy (= Socrates) will rule and make a permanent place for itself.

One generation later, Aristotle develops an ethical conception in which the virtuous person is, in his every act, implicitly or explicitly answering Socrates' fundamental question. The person of practical wisdom (the *phronimos*) is always and everywhere answering the question of how to live. The question which a generation ago was so disruptive of life is now the expression of ethical life itself. Here we have an example at the cultural level of the installation of a capacity: ethical culture can again function according to established patterns and paradigms. (This would be an example of responding to Socratic disruption by installing the ethical-cultural capacity to function again according to the reality principle, which itself is only a variant of the pleasure principle.)

At the end of the *Nicomachean Ethics,* Aristotle insists that we need laws to protect the possibility of a contemplative life. Rather than killing Socrates by a lawful, democratic vote, one should form a polis that protects by law the possibility of a Socrates. A Socratic life is no longer disruptive to society, but is normalized by it. (Of course, there are shifts. Aristotle isolates and focuses on the completely *impractical* life of contemplation, whereas Socrates was concerned with the practical question of how to live. But the general point remains: the laws must make the world safe for philosophy.) Indeed, by the end of the *Ethics,* the idea of a society which protects, and even honors, the philosophical life is starting to emerge as the conservative option. For, after all, it is the standard ethical virtues which, when reflected upon, point to the contemplative life as the best of all.

So here we see instantiated what, by now, should be a familiar pattern:

1. established forms of mental or cultural activity functioning according to the pleasure principle and reality principle (ancient Athenian culture)
2. active disruption (the life and death of Socrates)
3. attempts to heal over that disruption with creative activity (Plato's and Aristotle's invention of ethics and philosophy; the injection of a fundamental enigmatic signifier into life and the organization of a new form of life around it)
4. new established forms of mental or cultural activity functioning according to the pleasure principle and reality principle (philosophical culture, western civilization)

Aristotle's ethics and Freud's account of mental functioning can really capture only stages (1) and (4). They can capture a certain form of mental (cultural) activity once it has been established, but they have no account of the disruption and creativity that makes that form of mental (cultural) activity possible. Both thinkers have an intimation that there must be a "beyond"—a "beyond" to the ethical, a "beyond" to established forms of mindedness—but neither can adequately capture what that is.

3

THE REMAINDER OF LIFE

According to Aristotle, the goal of all human striving is happiness; according to Freud, "the aim of all life is death." In each case, as we have seen, there is something disruptive to the system, something which the system cannot itself contain. The mistake would be to think that our task is to think of *another principle* that would at last capture this leftover. That would be to engage in a repetition. For it is precisely the invocation of a principle that allows the formation of a conception of a "beyond." And the pressure that this system cannot contain then gets partially expressed in a fantasy of getting to this "beyond."[1] In each of the cases we have considered, we cannot get to "the remainder of life" directly. Rather, we glimpse it obliquely by working through an attempt to subsume human striving under a principle—and seeing how it fails. So if there is such a thing as "living life without remainder," it is likely that it will be achieved not by finally finding a principle which captures that remainder, but by finding acceptable ways of living without a principle. We would then no longer be in the business of creating a "beyond." And we would no longer be trying to explain the mind's self-disruptiveness with an overarching principle.

What would such a life be like? This is a tricky question to answer, for if we provide too much detail, we run the risk of providing yet another principle of human life. Nevertheless, I think we can at least sketch a picture of a mind that is functioning with an inherent tendency toward disruption—and not thereby commit ourselves to that disruption's being the expression of an overarching principle. And, having done that, we can then approach the history of psychoanalytic theorizing as though we were analyzing the resistances to this insight. The beauty of analyzing resistances is that it opens up all sorts of possibilities that cannot be anticipated. We do not complete our sketch by filling in more detail, but by clearing away blockages to our theorizing about the mind. Hopefully, we thereby become freer to understand the mind instead of imposing rigid frameworks upon it. In this way, psychoanalysis can free itself up by applying its own techniques to itself. It is to these two projects that I now turn.

So, first, a sketch of a self-disrupting mind.

At the end of his career, Freud wrote an essay that attempted to sum up the successes and failures of psychoanalysis. In "Analysis Terminable and Interminable," Freud brings us back to something which was there at the birth of psychoanalysis but which, Freud thinks in retrospect, was unjustly ignored in its development: quantity: "for the most part, our theoretical concepts have neglected to attach the same importance to the *economic* line of approach as they have to the *dynamic* and *topographical* ones . . . I am drawing attention to this neglect."[2] This neglect is remarkable because, as Freud points out, quantities of energy will always be there to overwhelm the mind's defenses, whether primitive or sophisticated. Repression is one of the mind's most primitive and pervasive defenses against the unwanted and the intolerable, but, Freud now says, it is of limited value as a defense against quantity. "Repressions behave like dams against the pressure of water . . . reinforcements may be set up by fresh traumas, enforced frustrations, or the collateral influence of instincts upon one another. The result is always the same, and it *underlines the irresistible power of the quantitative factor in the causation of illness*."[3]

Freud says that one of the aims of analysis is to "replace repressions that are insecure by reliable ego-syntonic controls", but even when that has been done, we "do not always achieve our aim to its full extent":

> *it is always a question of the quantitative factor, which is so easily overlooked* . . . analysis, in claiming to cure neuroses by ensuring control over instinct, is always right in theory, but not always right in practice. And this is because it does not always succeed in ensuring to a sufficient degree the foundations on which a control of instinct is based. The cause of such a partial failure is easily discovered. In the past, the quantitative factor of instinctual strength opposed the ego's defensive efforts; for that reason we called in the work of analysis to help; and now that same factor sets a limit to the efficacy of this new effort. *If the strength*

of the instinct is excessive, the mature ego, supported by analysis, fails in its task, just as the helpless ego failed formerly.[4]

"Just as the helpless ego failed formerly": the breaking down of an analytic cure is itself a repetition of the early failures of the "helpless ego." From a psychoanalytic point of view, this is the deepest form of human helplessness: helplessness in the face of too much energy. As Freud points out, we are vulnerable to repetitions of such helplessness from the beginning to the end of our lives. But this is a peculiar kind of "repetition"—because it is a repetition of something that is in itself without content. It is the breaking-through of quantity without quality. It is not a repetition of "helplessness," as though helplessness were the *content* of the experience—as when one *feels* helpless, overwhelmed, anxious; it is, rather, just helplessness breaking out again. Whether it becomes a repetition, in the psychoanalytic sense of a repetition compulsion, depends on what happens next. What appear as repetition are the mind's attempts, at varying levels of failure and success, to inform this breakthrough with meaning.

From a psychoanalytic point of view, there are two distinct senses in which life is too much. First, there is the structural insight that life is lived under conditions of tension. For the mind to discharge all its tension, to achieve a completely unpressured state, is precisely what it is for it to die. This was Freud's structural insight in *Beyond the Pleasure Principle*. In this sense, it is basically a structural truth that life is too much.[5] Second, because we are always and everywhere living under pressure, we must live with the possibility of a breakthrough in any psychological structure

109

we have thus far achieved. In part, this is due to the fact that psychological structure is itself a psychological achievement. It is a response to previous experiences of loss and gain—and as such is constitutionally vulnerable. Even a healthy ego—the ego of an Aristotelian virtuous person—is not proof against all possible onslaughts from within or without. There is no such thing as an ego that is invulnerable to trauma. And in actual life, the psychological achievements of maturity do tend to be somewhat fragile. There is always and everywhere the possibility of being overwhelmed.

In his programmatic 1914 paper "On Narcissism: An Introduction," Freud suggests that one way to avoid being overwhelmed is to fall in love.

At this point, our curiosity will of course raise the question why this damming-up of libido in the ego should have to be experienced as unpleasurable. I shall content myself with the answer that unpleasure is always the expression of a higher degree of tension, and that therefore what is happening is that a quantity in the field of material events is being transformed here as elsewhere into the psychical quality of unpleasure . . . Here we may even venture to touch on the question of what makes it necessary at all for our mental life to pass beyond the limits of narcissism and to attach the libido to objects. The answer which would follow from our line of thought would once more be that this necessity arises when the cathexis of the ego with libido exceeds a certain amount. A strong egoism is a pro-

tection against falling ill, *but in the last resort we must begin to love in order not to fall ill, and we are bound to fall ill if, in consequence of frustration, we are unable to love.*[6]

Freud then quotes the poet Heine, who gives us God's view of the Creation: "Illness was no doubt the final cause of the whole urge to create. By creating, I could recover, by creating, I became healthy." On this view, the world itself is God's way of avoiding trauma.

There is a question whether this "too much" should be conceptualized as outside or inside the mind. The temptation to view this energy as coming from outside is that it is in itself without quality: thus the image of pure energy impinging on the mind from the outside. This is a temptation which, I think, should be resisted. As we have just seen, the idea that the mind functions under conditions of "too much" is internal to the very idea of mindedness. What the mind is either dealing with or failing to deal with is mental energy. But how could energy be *mental* energy if it is in itself without quality, if it serves to break up the established structures of mind? Isn't it inherent in the mental that there be some content? Certainly, it is true that the very idea of mental energy derives from a recognition that psychological life has varying degrees of intensity. We experience ideas as pressing on us, and as fading away in importance. For Freud, the fundamental mental molecule was an idea-plus-quota of energy (which he called affect). It was the transfer of this energy along varying paths of ideas that allowed Freud to explain the formation of neurotic symptoms and dreams. In this use, psychic energy seems to be the "matter" of a form-and-matter unity. But, then, how could there be a case of pure, formless matter? How could there be *mental* energy without an idea? I think the answer is to take this as a limiting case of the mental—somewhat analogous to treating zero as a number. The reason for doing this is to capture the phenomena of trauma and of momentary breakthroughs: these are vicissitudes of the mental.

Now once we conceive of this excess of energy as mental, we have reason to think of the mind as a *self*-disrupting organism. But it is crucial not to think of this self-disruption as serving a teleological purpose. Again it is helpful to invoke Darwin. Darwin explained away the appearance of teleology by showing that although disruptions in nature may be occasions for the evolution of the species, that is not why they are occurring. Similarly, a disruption in the mind may be an occasion for growth, but that is not why it is occurring. The fact that there is a disruption is simply one manifestation of the fact that the mind lives in conditions of excess. It is not a special teleological property of the mind.

We should think of this self-disruptive force as *before* good and evil. It tends to break through established psychic structures and thus presents itself as a possibility for new possibilities. This, I suspect, is the deepest reading of human helplessness: humans are constitutionally unable to keep things fixed and forever immune to disruption and change. It is too metaphysical—in the pejorative sense of that term—and too misleading to call this force an "aggressive drive." We would be straying too far from our ordinary uses of "aggression." The breakthrough may be an occasion for aggression; it may even be a vehicle of aggression—as when

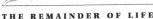

the mind uses these breakthroughs to attack its own mental functioning.[7] But we are presuming too much to call it aggressive: this energy has no inherent properties; it is just the "too much" of the system breaking through.

There is an important difference between saying that aggression is fundamental to human life (a significant empirical claim) and saying that it flows from a fundamental aggressive force. The latter claim does not follow from the former. One might at first think that one can make a simple appeal to evolutionary theory to justify the claim for an aggressive drive; but that is not so. It may well be that aggression is selected for—that it is the sufficiently aggressive humans who have been able to kill off the less aggressive ones and reproduce their kind. It does not follow that there is a basic aggressive force. Here is an alternative hypothesis: aggression emerges from a breakdown in the mind's efforts to make meaning —that is, a breakdown which cannot be healed by subsequent efforts to make meaning. This is certainly the aggression one sees acted out in the traumatic neuroses. In that case, what would be selected for would not be an aggressive drive per se but, rather, a certain incapacity to make meaning. Those who couldn't continue to make meaning would tend to kill off those who could.

The breakthrough, then, may be an occasion for aggression, but it may also be an occasion for creativity and growth. It may also occasion nothing at all, just a momentary interruption in the ordinary flow of mental activity. There is no good reason to call creativity in itself "aggressive" unless one is already searching for overarching principles—and there are two good reasons not to. First, it is a discovery of psychoanalysis that creativity often is aggressive—in the sense that it is the outcome of an oedipal strug-gle.[8] And, of course, there are important moments of creativity that do involve obvious attacks on established structures. One flattens these distinctions among types of creativity if one legis-lates that creativity by its very nature is "aggressive." Second, one runs the danger of turning "aggression" into an enigmatic signi-fier. In its most obvious meaning, we think of aggression as an at-tempt at destruction, creativity as an attempt at creation. Of course, it may well be a "philosophical" insight that creativity in-volves aggression and that aggression provides an occasion for creativity.[9] But as we move toward making this point, we are also moving toward the limits of language's ability to express coherent thought—and we run the risk of introducing a term that only ap-pears to mean something.

It now seems that we should distinguish two fundamentally dif-ferent types of unconscious mental activity. The first type I shall call *swerve*. This is the ordinary primary-process mental function-ing according to the pleasure principle. I call it swerve because we know of it mainly through the perturbations it causes within the realm of conscious experience: dreams, slips of the tongue, symptomatic acts. Because of swerve, there is no such thing as unproblematically inhabiting the space of reasons. In extreme cases, a person may, say, be afraid to go outside, though he is aware of no danger; but even in ordinary life there are countless occasions on which we find ourselves correcting distortions in our thinking—as when we recognize that all the efforts we have been putting into getting that new car, new house, new job, new man, new woman could not possibly yield the happiness we have been anticipating. The space of reasons is always and everywhere susceptible to being bent out of shape.

The second type is *break:* these are disruptions of primary-process mental activity itself, and they may also serve to disrupt secondary process. These breaks do not themselves function according to the pleasure principle, though whether they are "beyond" it is another matter. These breaks may remain just that: if they are massive, they are traumas; if they are small, they are *petits morts:* little breaks in the flow of mental activity. Often they go unnoticed. These breaks can become meaningful in one of two ways. Sometimes a break in the fabric of meaning will itself be meaningful simply by virtue of the context in which the break occurs—as, for instance, when a story is cut short. (One example of this is when a burst of anxiety wakes one from a dream. Another is when one continues to sleep but there is a sudden break in the dream.) It may well be that the break provides the story with a different meaning from the one it would have had were it allowed to unfold. This is not because of any inherent meaning in the break itself, but because of the context in which it occurs. In this way the break gains meaning parasitically on the particular fabric of meaning that it rips. At other times the mind will quickly rush in to supply the break with a meaning.

This distinction between swerve and break is, I think, essential to understanding the analytic process. Let me illustrate this by returning to a clinical vignette from my analytic practice: the analysand who inhabited a disappointing world. In addition to its symptoms, neurosis tends to be organized by a core unconscious fantasy. For this analysand, every instance of social recognition was interpreted by her as falling short of what she really deserved, as given to her only out of pity, as a disguised insult, and so on. All of this is an example of swerve, and it had the overall effect of creating an unconscious teleological structure: "the aim of life is disappointment."

In the analysis, this person developed an erotic transference and it took the shape of disappointment. Why, she asked, wouldn't I just make love to her on the couch? But it was just as well I was her analyst, she figured, because otherwise I would have to tell her straight out that I didn't love her. Anyway, how could I love anyone who had the same boring dreams over and over? "You must be rolling your eyes," she said as she recounted a familiar dream. She speculated that even after the analysis was over, I wouldn't date her . . . and so on.

She was a tad short-sighted, and about a year into the analysis she started using her short-sightedness to this advantage: *everywhere* she went she would see me with another woman. I am of medium height and build, with medium-length brown hair: in other words, if you are shortsighted, I can easily be mistaken for much of the male population. Unless you practice analysis yourself, it is hard to believe the level of anger an obvious transference distortion can provoke. There were occasions when she would come into my office in a bitter fury, because she had just seen me flirting with a woman outside. (The idea that it couldn't have been me, because I was already inside my office, waiting for her, was not something she could, at that moment, entertain.)

This analysand had an early-morning hour, and as she drove

into town each morning she began to develop the following habit. She knew I drove a blue Toyota—she had once seen me park it near my office—and now every time she saw a blue Toyota parked on the street, she knew that I was having an affair with some woman and was spending the night with her. Since there were, in those days, a fair number of blue Toyotas in town, I was having quite an active sex life—and yet I still wouldn't have an affair with her!

All of the above I consider to be a manifestation of swerve. No doubt there were many little breaks during the elaboration of this picture, but the overall transference was one in which love swerved to disappointment. But about three years into the analysis an important break occurred. She was driving into town, saw "my" blue Toyota, and suddenly said, "That's crap!" She surprised herself with her own exclamation. She came in and reported to me what happened in the ten minutes between that exclamation and the beginning of the session. Having said that to herself, she found herself somewhat disturbed and vigilant. And then she noticed *another* blue Toyota. Obviously, I couldn't be there too. And then she realized that she had been jealous *for years* and yet had not done anything to find out which blue Toyota was mine.

I take this to be an instance of break—and of the elaboration that can follow on from a break. I don't want to pretend that this break came from nowhere. I suspect that three years of analytic work had sufficiently loosened a neurotic structure that such a break became possible. In other words, I don't think that break is the beginning of analysis; it may itself be the outcome of shifts in

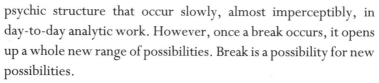

psychic structure that occur slowly, almost imperceptibly, in day-to-day analytic work. However, once a break occurs, it opens up a whole new range of possibilities. Break is a possibility for new possibilities.

The breakthrough I am describing was the first emotion-filled moment of clarity in the analysand's life in which she could see clearly that she was not the perpetual victim of disappointment. She could see herself creating her own experiences of disappointment. It is difficult to describe what a revolutionary insight this can be. In part, this is because terms like "victim" and "passivity" have become psychobabble: it is hard to live outside cliché when one comes anywhere near these words. But here goes: this person had lived her life as though disappointment were reality. It was happening *to* her, and she could not prevent it. It came as the most stunning reversal for her to realize that it wasn't the world imposing its disappointments on her, but her actively striving for disappointment. Why did she work so hard to be unhappy? This became an urgent puzzle for her—and it began to radiate outward. She could now begin to see that it was she, not I, who was busy placing me with other women. And it was she who attributed to her boss a patronizing motive when she got a promotion. This moment of break (along with the analysis) opened up new possibilities. And much of the rest of the analysis was given over to exploring them.

It is because neuroses tend to express some form of structure—an idiosyncratic "ethics"—that breaks will attack it, as they attack any other structure in the mind.[10] The break does not occur for any purpose—it is not in the service of any higher prin-

ciple—and it is precisely for that reason that they provide a unique analytic opportunity. With the manifestations of swerve, the analyst may interpret the dreams and symptoms and thereby help the patient slowly gain insight into the world she inhabits, but in moments of break there is a rip in the world itself—and this makes room for a different kind of analytic moment.

This is not to say that swerve is neurotic and break is not. As I understand it, neurosis itself is self-disrupting. On the one hand, there will be a core organizing fantasy that will tend to get expressed in swervelike ways. On the other hand, the neurosis will disrupt itself with symptomatic breakthroughs. And some of these breaks will look like repetitions. Neurosis, then, will both diffuse energy through its elaborated core fantasy *and* allow for momentary breakthroughs in which there is a burst of discharge. Neurosis, then, is a pathological form of regulating the buildup of energy both by diffusing and by discharging it. Thus it is a mistake to think that swerve is always neurotic, break always psychotic. Rather, these are distinctions in types of mental functioning that cut across diagnostic categories.

The distinction between swerve and break truly is *before good and evil*. There is no implicit assumption that moments of break are "good," paths of swerve "bad." On this occasion, a break was put to good analytic use, but one cannot generalize across the board. I emphasize this because there is, I think, a tendency for psychotherapeutic concepts to carry an implicit morality. So, for example, there is a widespread assumption among psychotherapists that "psychic synthesis" is good, that "integration" is good. But any analyst who actually thinks about his clinical practice will recognize that one of the most synthetic functions of the mind is neurosis. A high-functioning neurotic will "heal over" all sorts of breaks in neurotic structure by further elaborating the neurosis. Some neuroses have remarkable integrative powers—and that is why they are so stable.

Conversely, although breaks may provide an occasion for growth—as in the example above—they may also be occasions of massive destruction. When I worked at the veterans' hospital, I had a schizophrenic patient who once said to me, "Everything was all right until my life left me." Unlike a neurotic slip of the tongue, this utterance conveyed a psychotic truth. In fantasy, this person had placed his own soul inside the body of his wife. And when she left the trailer, he fell into a catatonic trance. This is an instance of what Melanie Klein calls projective identification.[11] In this fantasy, the mind has actively disrupted itself—a "piece" of mental functioning has "gone missing"—and the mind tries to represent that loss in terms of the forcible ejection of bodily substance. In projective identification there is an actual break in the mind—the mind is altered—which the mind tries to elaborate with psychotic content.

In short, a psychotic break is also a form of break. At first, it may be difficult to conceptualize the momentary disruption of neurotic structure and the massive psychotic disruption of the mind as two (different) instances of the same phenomenon. I suspect part of the difficulty lies in the fact that we are used to conceptualizing therapy in implicitly teleological terms. Thus there is a tendency to assume that break must be "good" or "bad." How can instances of the same thing be "good" and "bad"? We have just seen how. If we truly abandon any hidden commitment to teleology, we can then see that a wide range of phenomena—differing not only in intensity, but also in effect—can all be treated as instances of break.

To bring this point home, I offer a reinterpretation of a famous moment in one of Freud's case histories, that of the Rat Man.[12]

Things soon reached a point at which, in his dreams, his waking fantasies and his associations, he began heaping the grossest and filthiest abuse upon me and my family, though in his deliberate actions he never treated me with anything but the greatest respect. His demeanor as he repeated these insults to me was that of a man in despair. "How can a gentleman like you, sir," he used to ask, "let yourself be abused in this way by a low, good-for-nothing fellow like me? You ought to turn me out: that's all I deserve." While he talked like this, he would get up from the sofa and roam about the room,—a habit which he explained at first as being due to delicacy of feeling: he could not bring himself, he said, to utter such horrible things while he was lying there so comfortably. But soon he himself found a more cogent explanation, namely, that he was avoiding my proximity for fear of my giving him a beating. If he stayed on the sofa he behaved like someone in desperate terror trying to save himself from castigations of terrific violence; he would bury his head in his hands, cover his face with his arm, jump up suddenly and rush away, his features distorted with pain, and so on. He recalled that his father had had a passionate temper, and sometimes in his violence he had not known where to stop.[13]

Freud and the Rat Man agree on a "cogent" interpretation of this bizarre moment: the Rat Man is afraid that Freud is about to give him a beating. But there is a serious problem with this interpretation: other than the cringe itself, there is no evidence that the Rat Man is afraid of Freud. Certainly, the Rat Man does not *consciously* believe that Freud is a dangerous figure; he does not *consciously* believe that a trained doctor, working in his capacity as a psychoanalyst, is about to fly into uncontrollable rage. Now it is part of the logic of fear that to be afraid of X one must also believe that X poses some kind of threat. Thus there is conceptual pressure to say that the Rat Man must *unconsciously* believe that Freud is a danger. But beliefs do not exist in isolation.[14] For the Rat Man to have a single belief that Freud is a danger, he must have other beliefs about why Freud is a threat.

By now, I hope you are beginning to feel uncomfortable. For the logic of fear and the logic of belief are pressuring us to conceptualize the unconscious as being more structured and rational than it is. And there does not seem to be any clinical need for this. Certainly, the Rat Man is in some kind of panicked state, and we do need to capture that panic; but there is no need to interpret him as being in such a complex psychological state as "afraid that Freud is going to beat him." Indeed, such an interpretation contributes to the Rat Man's self-misunderstanding—and it does so precisely by confusing a break with swerve.

The situation, as I picture it, is this: as the analysis progresses, the transference has been deepening. There is a correlative build-up of anxiety. In this instance, the anxiety is building up around the Rat Man's open expression of aggression. Obsessional defenses are generally in place in order to control and contain aggression. So, in the open insults and abuse which the Rat Man hurls onto Freud, we are also witnessing a weakening and potential breakdown of obsessional structure. The "too much" is getting to be too much for the Rat Man to handle with his normal obsessional defenses. At this point, there is a break. The Rat Man experiences this break in terms of a brutal projective fantasy in which an internal, superego figure—the punishing "Rat Dad"—is projected out onto Freud. The result: a cringe before the externalized superego. What we see here is not so much a reaction of fear of Freud—or fear of his father—as it is a display of *intra*psychic structure spread out in social space. What we are seeing dramatized is the structure of the Rat Man's mind.[15] The Rat Man has organized his entire life so as to live in a cringe, and here we see a display of the core fantasy.

If we ignore the vicissitudes of mind, what we see will look like the Rat Man cringing in fear of Freud. It is precisely this social appearance which the Rat Man latches onto when he formulates his "more cogent explanation." It is typical for an obsessional to portray himself as more rational than he is. That is why the problem with his "more cogent explanation" is precisely that it is more cogent. This is a moment in which the Rat Man's obsessional structure is breaking up before Freud's eyes, and Freud basically joins the Rat Man in repairing it. That is, Freud here collaborates

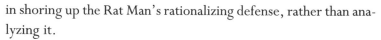

in shoring up the Rat Man's rationalizing defense, rather than analyzing it.

Perhaps in the specific case of the Rat Man, this was the right sort of therapeutic intervention. Perhaps the Rat Man was such a fragile figure that instead of analyzing his defenses, Freud was right in helping to shore them up. I wouldn't know. The point though is that this moment represents a significant break from the Rat Man's normal modes of obsessional functioning. The Rat Man has experienced a moment of break, and he is now in the process of covering it over with a rationalizing interpretation. Because he is unaware of the distinction between swerve and break, Freud unwittingly collaborates with an obsessional defense. This, I think, is a missed analytic opportunity.

Because at this moment the analyst is, as it were, a guest in the analysand's mind, there is room for him to participate in the creation of new possibilities. At this moment, the possibility for new possibilities has taken a peculiar shape: Freud has been given the voice of the Rat Dad. It is not that Freud should speak in this role, but he should understand that whatever he says will, at least in the first instance, be heard from this position. It is precisely at such a moment that the analysand moves *from* a position of being able to gain some (limited) insight into his psychological structure *to* a position of being able to change that structure.

This is a delicate moment. Because there has been a momentary breakdown in structure, there is room to move in all sorts of directions—some of them awful. In a negative therapeutic reaction—to take one horrific example—the analysand cannot listen to the analyst's interpretations. Rather, he treats them as objects and brutally introjects them, causing more and more breaks in his own mind. By inducing repeated disruptions, an analysand can break his own mind apart. The patient splits his mind into bits. I interpret this, following Melanie Klein, as the height of envy: mind brutally attacking its own existence.

Given that this, too, lies within the realm of possibility, I think one can see why Freud instinctively rushed to help the Rat Man repair his obsessional defenses. But one can also see that there were transformative possibilities he missed because he did not himself clearly distinguish a swerve from a break.

Now let us look for the moment to our own transformative possibilities. Once one distinguishes swerve from break, one ought to become skeptical of a current fashion in which the aim of psychoanalysis is purportedly to help the analysand construct a narrative of his life. The problem with narratives is that they tend to cover over breaks. They aim for a kind of coherence that often isn't there. And thus they often serve as a defense against recognizing some of the most active moments of mental life. Insofar as one has constructed a narrative, the mind will typically disrupt that structure too. And how is a narrative to contain an account of its own disruption? I suppose this is not impossible, but in actual analytic practice it is unlikely. In general, the attempts to construct a narrative serve to shore up the analysand's rationalizing defense. They cover over the countless breaks in which life opens up or breaks apart—and they calm the analyst's anxiety about whether she is really accomplishing something.

What, then, should an analyst do at a moment of break? I do not think one can give any general technical advice, beyond "notice that a break has occurred and think about what to do in relation to that." The reason is that each break will occur in the context of an analysis—in the context of a psychic unfolding—and the meaning of the break will depend on the context in which it occurs. In the case of the "disappointed analysand" I have been describing, it seemed appropriate to facilitate a process in which she could recover a sense of strangeness in her own activity. She had become puzzled and intrigued by her own behavior, and—in contrast to Freud's treatment of the Rat Man—I was concerned that she not rush to find "a more cogent explanation." Thus I avoided interpretations, and allowed her simply to pursue her own puzzlement. At moments when she got stuck, I might ask a question. So, for instance, when she herself expressed surprise that she could have simply assumed that each blue Toyota she saw was mine, I asked, "Did you ever think of checking license plates?" This evoked a smile, a pause, and a kind of concession that is difficult to describe. At some level of experience, she knew that she was allowing a drama to unfold, but somehow that "knowing" never really got in the way—at least, until the break.[16] At moments like this, interpretation is, I think, inappropriate, for one should not here want to capture how things fit together. Rather, this is a moment for the analysand to experience vividly how she has managed to live with things not fitting together.

Once one grasps the self-disrupting character of mind, one is in a position to appreciate a claim that is strange but true: psychoanalysis does not promote virtue, but it does promote happiness. From an Aristotelian perspective, such a claim appears paradoxi-

cal, for the virtues are precisely those traits of character that do promote happiness. But by now it should be clear why the dream of an expanded Aristotelian approach to ethics which took the unconscious into account is just that: a dream. The unconscious is not simply an extra realm of desires. And so we cannot just take some hidden desires into account as we figure out how to live. The unconscious includes certain self-disrupting tendencies that cannot be so contained.

At first, one might well think that in a psychoanalytic therapy one is being habituated: one is being habituated into a kind of analytic mindedness. One develops the skill of paying attention to the flow of one's own thoughts, of associating fairly freely to them, and of paying attention when there are blocks or slips. One learns how to make interpretations of one's own slips, dreams, and symptomatic acts. Why isn't this a virtue?

I think we can see why not if we compare the analytically minded person to the person of practical wisdom in Aristotle's *Ethics,* the *phronimos.* The *phronimos* is always referring the unfolding events back to the relevant virtue; he is always implicitly answering the question of whether this is an occasion for courage or for kindness.[17] Thus although this may be an adaptive life, a healthy life, a life with complexity, nuance, and ingenuity in it, it will nevertheless bear the structure of repetition. The *phronimos* interprets experience in terms of the ethical virtues, and the ethical virtues are structures of repetition. But the unconscious attacks structures of repetition—even its own.

The analytically minded person—in contrast to the *phronimos* —takes advantage of breaks in the structures. Instead of referring the break back to a structure of repetition—this is, in effect, what the Rat Man and Freud do when they treat the cringe as fear—one treats it as an occasion for opening up new possibilities, possibilities not included in any established structure. In this sense, analysis begins when the analysand *declines* the role of *phronimos*—and branches off in ways that do not fit any established virtue. Of course, any such breaking-open is typically followed by a return to the old order: that is one reason why analysis is such a slow business. And to return to the position of *phronimos* may be the healthiest form of return. But analytic mindedness is not a constituent virtue of the *phronimos;* in this sense it is a departure from the ethical. It stands in a similar position with respect to the ethical virtues as Aristotle's contemplation did. It is, as it were, an existential sabbath from ethical life.

Freud himself comes pretty close to saying that there can be no psychoanalytic equivalent to the *phronimos*. In "Analysis Terminable and Interminable," Freud asks whether an analysis should end when the actual conflicts which the patient presents have been treated or whether it should aim for "absolute psychical normality." In this imagined ideal, the analysis would have "such a far-reaching influence on the patient that no further change could be expected to take place in him if his analysis were continued."[18] Freud seems to treat it as a limitation of psychoanalysis that it can only treat actual problems as they arise and is incapable of providing a cure for all possible problems. Of course, if there were such a state of "absolute psychical normality," this would be the condition of the psychoanalytic *phronimos:* the person of psychological wisdom. That there can be no such person is not, *contra* Freud, a

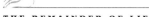
limitation of psychoanalysis so much as it is a celebration of human possibility. It is a consequence of Freud's own views that, in human life, possibilities for new possibilities are breaking out all the time. It is not an empirical limitation but a matter of logic that psychoanalysis cannot treat them until they become actual.

But if psychoanalysis lies outside the ethical, how does it promote happiness? Here we need to go back to an older English usage of "happiness" in terms of happenstance: the experience of chance things' working out well rather than badly. Happiness, on this interpretation, is not the ultimate goal of our teleologically organized strivings, but the ultimate ateleological moment: a chance event going well for us—quite literally, a lucky break. Analysis puts us in a position to take advantage of certain kinds of chance occurrences: those breaks in psychological structure which are caused by too much of too much. This isn't a teleological occurrence, but a taking-advantage of the disruption of previous attempts to construct a teleology. If one thinks about it, I think one will see that in such fleeting moments we do find real happiness.

Of course, psychoanalysis is concerned with large-scale changes in psychological structure, not merely with these moments of break. But what is involved in large-scale change? What happens, say, when it emerges that a person no longer has to inhabit a disappointing world? Or when a person is no longer constrained by a cruel superego? Or when a person can begin to live a more imaginative, vibrant, and happy life—a life in which she draws on unconscious wishes as a source of creativity rather than an occasion for fear and inhibition? What has opened up in each case is a new field of possibilities. In a disappointing world, for example, disappointments are all the possibilities there are. But when that world itself fades away, a person finds herself in a new field. Now much slow and painstaking analytic work is involved in opening up this space, but much of that progress occurs in working through the significance of moments of break. Implicitly analysts have been doing this all along: paying close attention to slips of the tongue, sentence constructions that get broken off before the sentence is complete, trains of thought that get interrupted, and so on. These moments of break are possibilities for new possibilities. And psychoanalysis is the art of taking advantage of lucky breaks.

Thus far I have been trying to give a sketch of how we might think of a self-disrupting mind in a nonprincipled way. I should now like to turn to an analysis of the resistances. The resistance I should like to consider in some detail is what I shall call *the metaphysics of aggression*.

Freud should have concluded from his ruminations in *Beyond the Pleasure Principle* that the kind of exceptions to the pleasure principle that concerned him didn't need another principle to explain them, but a theoretical willingness to tolerate a lack of principle. But instead of being willing to tolerate absence—that is, to live with a kind of theoretical anxiety—he tried to turn that absence into a presence by giving it a name, "death." Freud expresses surprise that it took him so long to do this: "I can no longer understand how we can have overlooked the ubiquity of non-erotic aggressivity and destructiveness and can have failed to give it its due place in our interpretation of life." This would sug-

gest that the history of psychoanalysis, until a certain break-through, is a history of ignoring nonerotic aggression. Retrospectively, he sees this inattention as motivated:

> I remember my own defensive attitude when the idea of an instinct of destruction first emerged in psychoanalytic literature, and how long it took before I became receptive to it. That others should have shown, and still show, the same attitude of rejection surprises me less. For "little children do not like it" when there is talk of the inborn human inclination to "badness," to aggressiveness and destructiveness, and so to cruelty as well. God has made them in the image of His own perfection; nobody wants to be reminded how hard it is to reconcile the undeniable existence of evil—despite the protestations of Christian Science—with His all-powerfulness or His all-goodness.[19]

Note that Freud is willing to attribute a motive to others, but though he acknowledges that he was defensive, he does not tell us the content of his defense. It is unlikely that he would see himself as trying to protect God's goodness. Here is my hypothesis: Freud overlooked aggression not because of an inherent aversion to looking at human wickedness, but because he had nothing to say about it. If one is trying to see the whole—somehow to capture the whole of human existence—one will be motivated to overlook what doesn't fit within that whole.

By 1920 Freud is ready to break up what he has come to see as a fantasied unity of mental functioning. The mind can no longer be understood in terms of the pleasure principle, but instead of living with the gap, he posits a "beyond." It is in this way that Freud takes himself to be explaining aggression. Aggression is now interpreted as the death drive diverted outward.[20] It is precisely this move which locks us into an inescapably negative teleology. Let us just assume (for the sake of argument, though I think it true) that humans are aggressive animals, and that dealing with human aggression is a serious psychological and social problem. The question remains: how might one deal with it? But if, as Freud does, one interprets aggression as the most obvious manifestation of one of the two primordial forces in the universe, the answer would seem to be: there is no successful way. My first inclination is to say that this leads to a pessimistic view of the human condition; but this isn't really the issue. My second inclination is to say it leads to a limited view of the human condition; but even this doesn't get to the heart of the problem. The point here is not to endorse an ontic optimism—that if we didn't adopt that view, we could shape life in nonaggressive ways—but to confront an ontological insight: that Freud's interpretation is an instance of bad faith. The metaphysical basicness of the death drive implies a kind of metaphysical intractability to the phenomenon of human aggression. As a matter of empirical fact, humans may be aggressive animals—and the fact of human aggression may be difficult to deal with. It may even be experienced as intractable. But to raise this purported intractability to a metaphysical principle is to obliterate the question of responsibility. And it is to cover over—by precluding—what might turn out to be significant empirical possibilities.

The most salient instance of this is Freud's claim that a punish-

ing superego is an inescapable product of civilization. The argument is as simple as it is elegant: Human aggression is the death drive turned outward; thus it is an inescapable vicissitude for any living creature. Therefore, for civilization to be possible, there must be a way for humans to contain their aggression, at least to the extent that they can live together. This requires a further vicissitude: that the aggression gets redirected inward. The superego is formed, and a person's aggression is channeled through it and thus directed onto his own ego. For Freud, this is the value of our civilized values: our values are vehicles of aggression against ourselves, by which we keep ourselves sufficiently in line to be able to live among others without killing them or being killed by them.

This formation leads to a horrific consequence: the more punishing the superego is, the more punishing it becomes. This is what Freud takes to be the distinctive contribution of psychoanalysis:

> conscience exhibits a peculiarity . . . which is no longer easy to account for. For the more virtuous a man is, the more severe and distrustful is its behaviour, so that ultimately it is precisely those people who have carried saintliness furthest who reproach themselves with the worst sinfulness. This means that virtue forfeits some part of its promised reward; the docile and continent ego does not enjoy the trust of its mentor, and strives in vain, it would seem to acquire it . . .
>
> Here at last an idea comes in which belongs entirely to psychoanalysis and which is foreign to people's ordinary

way of thinking . . . it tells us that conscience (or more correctly, the anxiety which later becomes conscience) is indeed the cause of instinctual renunciation to begin with, but that later the relationship is reversed. Every renunciation of instinct now becomes a dynamic source of conscience and every fresh renunciation increases the latter's severity and intolerance . . .

The effect of instinctual renunciation on the conscience then is that every piece of aggression whose satisfaction the subject gives up is taken over by the superego and increases the latter's aggressiveness (against the ego).[21]

The idea is simple: the more inhibited aggression is in direct expression, the more freed up it is to be used by the superego. That this is a familiar psychic configuration is, by now, beyond question. And that this formation is facilitated by Judeo-Christian culture—one which is built around internalization of the Law—also seems correct. But rather than see this as one configuration among other possible ones (along the lines of a neurotic solution to a conflict), Freud raises this configuration to inescapable ontology. There may be a question of more or less, but in Freud's view, civilization simply is the social manifestation of a certain configuration of human aggression.

It seems to me that a proper understanding of "the death drive"—or, rather, of what is important about "the death drive" —tilts one in a different direction. From a psychoanalytic perspective, human life is lived under conditions of tension. It is a condition of life that there is always too much tension for the mind

fully to metabolize. This is a structural point: living with this "too much" is what life is. The questions become: "How much is this 'too much?'" and "How well or badly is it tolerated?" Now given that there necessarily is "too much" for the mind to metabolize, there is always going to be energy available which could be deployed in breaking up the established structures of the mind. These are the breakthrough moments that Freud recognized as beyond the pleasure principle. (And it is this idea more than any other that links the structural point that the death drive discloses with an aggressive phenomenon.) But now if, for any structure, we will nevertheless be living with the possibility of such a breakthrough moment, then there *ought* to be the possibility of a break in the structure of punishing superego set over against a confined ego. No doubt this is an incredibly durable structure precisely because the superego can take up and express more and more energy. But the energy it takes up is the energy released from the ego as it becomes more and more inhibited. The larger picture, however, is that that entire dynamic is taking place in the context of an excess of energy that lies outside and continues to put pressure on the dynamic itself. Rather than see the aggressive superego as a clear manifestation of "the death drive," then, one should see it as one more psychological structure which "the death drive" might disrupt.

Freud doesn't see this because instead of treating "the death drive" as a permanent and peculiar possibility of mindedness, he substantializes it and turns it into a basic metaphysical principle. And he treats himself as passive in the face of his own thinking: "To begin with it was only tentatively that I put forward the views I have developed here, but in the course of time they have gained such a hold upon me that I can no longer think in any other way."[22] In retrospect one can see how Freud was seduced by his own thinking, for he treats the death drive as necessarily enigmatic: "it was not easy to demonstrate the activities of this supposed death instinct . . . It might be assumed that the death instinct operated silently within the organism towards its dissolution . . . two instincts seldom—*perhaps never*—appear in isolation from each other, but are alloyed with each other in varying and different proportions *and so become unrecognizable to our judgment.*"[23]

One wants to say, *of course* the death drive works in silence— not, however, because it is a mysterious principle, but because it is not a principle at all. It is, rather, a tendency expressed by the system as a whole. It is another way of expressing overall structural functioning: namely, that the mind is in the business of metabolizing and discharging tension and that it is always working under conditions of "too much." Freud mistakes a general tendency of the system for a teleological principle functioning in it— and thereby seduces himself with his own enigmatic signifier.[24]

Freud takes himself simultaneously to have explained human aggression—as an outward manifestation of the death drive—and to have confirmed the death drive by the phenomenon of human aggression. This may look like a pretty tight circle, but Freud justifies it with a fairly sophisticated appeal to the philosophy of science: his speculations, he says, explain the phenomena, and he can find no more serviceable or economical explanation. He declares himself happy to revise his hypothesis in the light of a better one.[25] The appeal to philosophy of science *is* sophisticated; the problem is that it is being invoked to allow Freud to rest with the assumptions with which he by now feels comfortable. What really gets secured here is the assumption that aggression is the expression of a basic metaphysical principle—and this adds a layer of ontological intractability to the problem of aggression.

On this view, the only relatively healthy thing we can do with our aggression is to become civilized. Yet civilization will necessarily make us feel "discontent." For Freud, the only choice is whether we take out our aggression on others or on ourselves. Inevitably we will do both; the question is one of balance. This is what leads Freud to what he calls his "astonishing" hypothesis: that what we call civilization is largely responsible for our suffering.[26] Actually, the hypothesis is far less astonishing if we treat this aspect of the civilization we inhabit along the lines of a neurotic solution to a real problem. There is no doubt that the organizing myths of the Judeo-Christian tradition facilitate the development of psychological structures that manifest a punishing superego and an unconscious sense of guilt.[27] But if one thinks of this as a neurotic structure, the question arises: are there nonneurotic forms of social organization? It also opens one to the recognition that "discontent" may not be directly attributable to civilization so much as to life itself. If it is a feature of life itself that it is lived under conditions of tension, that, as a condition of being alive there will always be "too much," then discontent becomes the expression of life itself. Civilization will inform that discontent, and there will be better and worse forms; but it is not to civilization as such that humans owe their discontent.

By positing the death drive as a metaphysical principle and

treating aggression as its most obvious manifestation, Freud traps himself into thinking that the actual structure of civilization that he isolated was the constituting condition of civilization itself. Every neurotic treats his world as the world; every neurotic treats his unconscious fantasies as giving him the entire universe of possibilities. In a similar fashion, Freud's penchant for teleological explanation led him to view a particular "solution" to the problem of aggression as the only one possible. The outcome was the view that in civilization suffering is inevitable. Again, it is a familiar feature of neurotic organization that the neurotic thinks he is passive in the face of suffering that is inevitably inflicted on him. Freud puts forward a similar view of the human condition in civilization.

On the surface it looks as though Freud is an antiteleological thinker, because, in contrast to Aristotle, he is clear that humans do not really fit into the universe:

> what decides the purpose of life is simply the programme of the pleasure principle. This principle dominates the operation of the mental apparatus from the start. There can be no doubt about its efficacy, and yet its programme is at loggerheads with the whole world, with the macrocosm as much as with the microcosm. There is no possibility at all of its being carried through; all the regulations of the universe run counter to it. One feels inclined to say that the intention that man should be "happy" is not included in the plan of "Creation."[28]

The human project of happiness is at loggerheads with the macrocosm because nature imposes deprivation and suffering, and soci-

ety inhibits desire. It is at loggerheads with the microcosm because, as we have seen, even within the human psyche there is
strong opposition to unconscious wishes as well as to conscious
desires. To view humans as striving for happiness is, from Freud's
perspective, to overlook one of the most salient facts about them:
they are always and everywhere tripping themselves up. And, for
Freud, it is precisely one's values, one's moral code, one's superego, which gets in the way of happiness. But it is important to
grasp the nature of the difference with Aristotle. It is not that
Aristotle is a teleological thinker and Freud is not, but that Aristotle sees humans as embedded in a harmonious structure, and
Freud sees humans as inevitably caught in the intersection of two
conflicting purposeful principles. "And now, I think, the meaning
of the evolution of civilization is no longer obscure to us. It must
present the struggle between eros and death . . . This struggle is
what all life essentially consists of."

Anyone who thinks it intelligible to inquire after the meaning
of civilization —and tries to answer that question by invoking two
purposeful principles which are alleged to rule the universe—is
not an antiteleological thinker. Freud sees hidden purpose everywhere; he just doesn't think that the purpose is there *for* humans.
The fact that, for Freud, humans are not made for happiness does
not place him outside the realm of teleological thinking.

In fact, it is here that Freud shows himself to be a tragic
thinker. For the ancient Greeks, tragic consciousness was constituted by the idea that humans are fated to live in the intersection
of two different realms of meaning, one human, the other divine.
Divine meaning can be understood at best obscurely and imper-

fectly, yet misunderstanding it could have profound, sometimes catastrophic consequences.[29] For Freud, of course, we are fated to live in the intersection of two conflicting realms of meaning, but the other realm—the unconscious—has, for the most part, been secularized and domesticated. I say "for the most part" because now all mental functioning is conceptualized as a human instantiation of two principles that are in themselves purposeful and transcendent. From a psychological perspective, one of the main values of a tragic consciousness is that it preserves a teleological outlook in the face of events that look rather horrid for human beings. The Greek tragedians were able to hold onto the idea that the world had a purpose, even if it wasn't a specifically human purpose. In a similar vein, Freud is able to hold onto the idea that all mental events are purposeful—even in the face of events that seem to attack and destroy the mind.

Freud says that the "common man" cannot imagine God otherwise than as an enormously exalted figure. "The whole thing is so patently infantile, so foreign to reality, that for anyone with a friendly attitude to humanity it is painful to think that the great majority of mortals will never be able to rise above this view of life." And yet he concludes that "the religion of the common man is the only religion which ought to bear that name."[30] By so confining religion to worship of the Father, might Freud be hiding from himself a certain religious turn in his own thinking? After all, he is attempting to provide a fundamental explanation of all mental phenomena by appeal to two cosmic, purposeful principles, transcending human life. Is not the idea that human life must inhabit a world governed by purposeful principles that influence life but also transcend it—is not this idea a religious one? But Freud's unconscious adherence to a metaphysics of aggression goes even deeper than postulating cosmic principles.

Let us consider Freud's analysis of the religion of the "common man." Freud takes himself to be uncovering the hidden roots of religious commitment, but if we look at his analysis *as itself the expression of a resistance,* what emerges is an irrational attachment to an unthought-out metaphysics. And it is one that, in hidden ways, still affects the practice of psychoanalysis. Freud, I think, had a hope that psychoanalysis could take the place of religion. That is, he thought that psychoanalysis provided a healthy and mature way to deal with typical fantasies and conflicts which had previously been expressed in religious myths. But if that is so, Freud's own fantasy about the nature of religious experience may well infect his understanding of the task of psychoanalysis. The question then becomes to what extent Freud's expectation that psychoanalysis would take the place of religion exercised a hidden and constraining influence on psychoanalysis itself. As we shall see, this is of a piece with the metaphysics of aggression.

In *Moses and Monotheism,* published in 1939, at the end of his career, Freud argues that Western civilization is founded on an actual act of aggression: the murder of Moses by the Hebrew people. He also argues that this murder left a permanent trace on the Jewish people—a "phylogenetic inheritance" which is passed along from one generation to the next. These two astonishing theses have left a trace on psychoanalysis itself.

According to Freud, there is no direct way Moses could have

succeeded in imposing monotheism on the Jews (or anyone else). Moses tried, but, according to Freud, the demands of monotheism were too arduous, and the Jewish people rose up, killed their leader, and then effaced any memory of the murder. And precisely by trying to kill off monotheism in *this* way, they forever branded it in their souls. The Jewish religion, according to Freud, *is* the memory of the murder, getting expressed in a hidden way—in the form of a shared obsessional neurosis. For Freud, only the *actual* murder of the father will usher in his symbolic return in the form of the Mosaic Law inscribed in the hearts and minds of the Jewish people.

Indeed, even the actual murder on its own would have been insufficient permanently to inscribe the religion: it had to serve as a reminder of a previous crime. According to Freud, we all live with an archaic memory of a primal crime that stands as the originating moment of civilization itself: the murder of the "primal father" by the sons. Instead of treating this as an organizing myth, Freud treats this murder as an actual event.[31] It is, as it were, the event which ushered in history. The idea is that in prehistory, society was held together by a "primal father" who had sexual access to all the women and who subjugated the sons and brothers. This was a fairly stable configuration in which, from a historical point of view, nothing happened. At some point the reigning primal father would become weak and would be murdered by the next strong man, and so it would go. History begins with the murder that makes a difference: the sons band together and kill the primal father, and, instead of one person taking over, they institute strict rules of exogamy. Now people are brought together in complex laws of marriage and exchange, and no one can ever again assume the position of primal father. From a Freudian perspective, history is the history of the incest taboo and its vicissitudes.

The murder of the father left a permanent mark on these first inhabitants of civilization. For the father who was hated was also a father who was loved, and once the hated father was removed, the other side of the ambivalence could come to the fore—and it did so in the form of guilt. The Jewish people occupy a special place in Western history because, in murdering Moses, they not only repeated the primal crime, but they did so on the leader who brought them monotheistic religion and the Ten Commandments. This brought about a historically specific and fateful cultural formation of guilt, the Jewish religion. Judaism, for Freud, has the structure of a shared obsessional neurosis which both hides and thereby expresses the murder of the father.

It would be worth while to understand how it was that the monotheist idea made such a deep impression precisely on the Jewish people and that they were able to maintain it so tenaciously. It is possible, I think, to find an answer. Fate had brought the great deed and misdeed of primaeval days, the killing of the father, closer to the Jewish people by causing them to repeat it on the person of Moses, an outstanding father-figure. It was a case of "acting out" instead of remembering, as happens so often with neurotics during the work of analysis. To the suggestion that they should remember, which was made to them by the doctrine of Moses, they reacted, however, by disavowing their action; they remained halted at the recognition of the great father and thus blocked their access to the point from which Paul was later to start his continuation of the primal history . . .

The killing of Moses by his Jewish people . . . thus becomes an indispensable part of our construction, an important link between the forgotten event of primaeval times and its later emergence in the form of monotheist religions. It is plausible to conjecture that remorse for the murder of Moses provided the stimulus for the wishful phantasy of the Messiah . . . who was to return and lead his people to redemption and the promised world-dominion. If Moses was this first Messiah, Christ became his substitute and successor, and Paul could exclaim to the peoples with some historical justification: "Look! the Messiah has really come: he has been murdered before your eyes!" *Then too there is a piece of historical truth in Christ's resurrection, for he was the resurrected Moses and behind him the returned primal father of the primitive horde, transfigured and, as the son, put in the place of the father.*

The poor Jewish people, who with their habitual stubbornness continued to disavow the father's murder, atoned heavily for it in the course of time. They were constantly met with the reproach "You killed our God!" And this reproach is true, if it is correctly translated. If it is brought into relation with the history of religions it runs: "you will not admit that you murdered God (the primal picture of God, the primal father, and his later reincarnations)." There should be an addition declaring: "We did

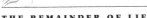

the same thing, to be sure, but we have admitted it and since then we have been absolved."[32]

On this interpretation, the Judeo-Christian tradition is the unfolding in a specific cultural form of the guilt surrounding the inaugurating act of civilization itself. But Freud is convinced that this tradition could not survive solely on the basis of its organizing myths, rituals, and practices. At bottom, there has to be a "phylogenetic heritage"—permanent traces of the original murder of the primal father, reinforced by subsequent traces of the murders of Moses and Christ. Freud, of course, did not have the language of genes and DNA, but if he had, I am sure he would have used it. The point is that the experience of a traumatic event made a phylogenetic difference—a difference that is passed on from generation to generation independently of the culture's rituals and myths. For Freud, there is a historical-biological basis to being a Jew. He thinks he gets evidence of this phylogenetic heritage from the ordinary psychoanalysis of individual neurotics.

A fresh complication arises when we become aware of the probability that what may be operative in an individual's psychical life may include not only what he has experienced himself but also things that were innately present in him at his birth, elements with a phylogenetic origin— an archaic heritage . . . When we study the reactions to early traumas, we are quite often surprised to find that they are not strictly limited to what the subject himself has really experienced but diverge from it in a way which fits in much better with the model of a phylogenetic event and, in general, can only be explained by such an influence. The behaviour of neurotic children towards their parents in the Oedipus and castration complex abounds in such reactions, which seem unjustified in the individual case and only become intelligible phylogenetically—by their connection with the experience of earlier generations. [The evidence is] strong enough for me to venture on a further step and to posit the assertion that the archaic heritage of human beings comprises not only dispositions but also subject-matter—memory-traces of the experience of earlier generations . . .

If we assume the survival of these memory-traces in the archaic heritage, we have bridged the gulf between the individual and group psychology: we can deal with peoples as we do with an individual neurotic. *Granted that at the time we have no stronger evidence for the presence of memory-traces in the archaic heritage than the residual phenomena of the work of analysis which call for a phylogenetic derivation,* yet this evidence seems to us strong enough to postulate that such is the fact. If it is not so, we shall not advance a step further along the path we entered on, either in analysis or in group psychology. *The audacity cannot be avoided . . .*

After this discussion I have no hesitation in declaring that men have always known (in this special way) that they once possessed a primal father and killed him.

. . . What is certainly of decisive importance, however, is the awakening of the forgotten memory-trace by a recent real repetition of the event. The murder of Moses was a repetition of this kind and later, the supposed judicial murder of Christ: so that these events come into the foreground as causes. It seems as though the genesis of monotheism could not do without these occurrences . . .

And lastly a remark which brings up a psychological argument. *A tradition that was based only on communication could not lead to the compulsive character that attaches to religious phenomena.* It would be listened to, judged, and perhaps dismissed, like any other piece of information from outside; it would never attain the privilege of being liberated from the constraint of logical thought. It must have undergone the fate of being repressed, the condition of lingering in the unconscious, before it is able to display such powerful effects on its return, to bring the masses under its spell, as we have seen with astonishment and hitherto without comprehension in the case of religious tradition. And this consideration weighs heavily in favour of our believing that things really happened in the way we have tried to picture them or at least in some similar way.[33]

This argument makes aggression and guilt into metaphysical principles. The memory of a primal aggression is inscribed in our souls; this memory helps to constitute who and what we are. Judaism and Christianity are, for Freud, culturally shared fantasies—but there is something prior to them: the aggression to which they are a response, and the guilt to which they give expression.

Put in this way, it becomes clear that this whole theoretical edifice is nothing other than the return of the seduction hypothesis—now applied at the level of civilization rather than at the level of the individual. That is, it is a return to the *latent content* of the seduction hypothesis: the idea that the appeal to a real-life event can be the explanatory end of the line. In 1897 Freud tried to give up the idea that individual neurosis was always and everywhere caused by an actual childhood event, a seduction; but in 1939 Freud cannot let go of the idea that cultural neurosis is caused by an actual event in the infancy of civilization, a murder. I see this move as a displacement. Freud is stuck: he has been seduced by the seduction hypothesis, and if he cannot apply it to the individual then he'll find something else to apply it to. Once Freud realizes that the fantasies that he has heard from individual patients are not actual accountings of real-life events, he comes to think that there must be some *other* real-life event which grounds and explains those fantasies: if not in this life, then in a previous life; if not in history, then in prehistory. It is as though in trying to abandon the seduction hypothesis, he can't quite let it go. It keeps coming back at a different level.[34]

I do not think it too strong to speak of Freud as "seduced" and "fixated," for the argument he gives for these astonishing conclusions are remarkably weak. As we have just seen, Freud himself admits that the only evidence he has for positing a "phylogenetic heritage" is the exaggerated and intractable phenomena that we find in an individual analysis. For example, an individual may display an intensity of guilt that goes beyond any appropriate reaction to anything that has happened in her life—and that guilt may be remarkably resilient and nonresponsive to treatment. But to say

that this is evidence for an archaic heritage is simply to deny the creative power of fantasy. For if one really does succeed in abandoning the seduction hypothesis, then this phenomenon of intense, intractable, and otherwise inexplicable guilt will then become evidence for the power and durability of certain organizing fantasies. To say that this phenomenon is evidence of archaic memory is to beg the question. For it is to say that this phenomenon cannot be accounted for on the basis of fantasy alone; and that is to say that it must be accounted for by a real event. But that just is the seduction hypothesis. In this way, Freud treats the seduction hypothesis as evidence for itself.

Similarly with Freud's claim that "a tradition that was based only on communication could not lead to the compulsive character that attaches to religious phenomena." Freud here assumes a dichotomy: either we can explain the tenacity of a culture by its ability to communicate across generations with readings, rituals, and other practices, or, if we can't, we have to assume a real historical event that was laid down in memory which supports those rituals. He then claims that the first option is not a real possibility and finds himself "forced" to conclude that there is a phylogenetic heritage. But this whole argument, weak as it is, is resting on a false dichotomy. There is a third possibility which the argument ignores: that a cultural tradition may tap and organize powerful unconscious fantasies. The tenacity of the religion would then not have to come from the cultural manifestations of the religion itself—rather, the tenacity of those manifestations would be explained by the powerful fantasies they helped to express.[35] By overlooking this possibility, Freud turns his back on the creative power of fantasy. In effect, he turns his back on one of the most important contributions of psychoanalysis to our understanding of human being.[36]

So, having grounded the hypothesis of a phylogenetic heritage in nothing stronger than its own postulation, Freud goes on to claim that Western civilization can be understood only in these terms. This claim may look preposterous and easily dismissable. One might be tempted to think that these ruminations on civilization can be treated as just that: they can be lopped off from the rest of psychoanalysis and treated as a speculative excess on Freud's part. This strategy won't work. For these claims seep into psychoanalysis itself, and they place significant constraints on how psychoanalysis treats aggression and guilt. One begins to see this hidden influence by considering how Freud interprets the relation between Judaism and Christianity, and the relation of both of these formations to psychoanalysis itself. For Freud, Christianity represents an important psychological advance over Judaism. For since, supposedly, there was a real historical murder, Judaism gets interpreted as a stubborn obsessional refusal to acknowledge it. The Jews are stuck expressing their guilt precisely because they cannot acknowledge it. Christianity represents an advance, rather than simply a different cultural configuration, because it does acknowledge (in mythical form) the real guilt derived from a series of real murders. Christians, unlike Jews, are not forever stuck in their guilt. Because they have acknowledged it, they are "saved"— that is, they are saved from being stuck in guilt and can move on. In this way, Christianity represents the religion of remembering, Judaism the religion of repetition.

The transformation of the soul that is involved in shifting from being an observant Jew to being a committed Christian is an example of what Freud has in mind when he speaks of "making the unconscious conscious." Obviously, this is no mere cognitive insight, the becoming aware of a fact one has previously not known. It involves, rather, a massive shift in one's ways of being. But this shift from committed Jew to committed Christian is, for Freud, a paradigm of becoming conscious of one's guilt. Of course, Christianity, like Judaism, remains a religion, and so it remains, for Freud, at best an infantile solution to a real problem. Although Christianity is a significant psychological advance over traditional Judaism, it nevertheless remains trapped in wishful fantasies of a loving and all-powerful Father. It was, Freud thought, the best humans could do two thousand years ago to acknowledge their guilt, but now we can do better.

Psychoanalysis, Freud thought, needed to be understood in the context of this movement of civilization. For it offered a thoroughly disillusioned—and thus completely secularized—way to acknowledge guilt. In this way, psychoanalysis represented as significant an advance over Christianity as Christianity had offered over Judaism. Psychoanalysis, like Christianity, offers the deep, soul-transforming ways of acknowledging guilt, but it does away with the illusion of an omnipotent and loving God. It has looked to many readers that *Moses and Monotheism* is an anti-Jewish book, but in fact it offers Jews a way of leapfrogging ahead of Christianity. This was an offer, Freud thought, that contemporary European Jews could not refuse. For although Judaism is a stuck religion, Jews themselves were becoming unstuck. In huge numbers, the Jews of post-Enlightenment Europe found they could no longer go on in the ways of their parents and grandparents. It is precisely in this context that Freud placed psychoanalysis. In Freud's view it offered civilization a way of preserving the best of Christianity while moving beyond religious commitment altogether. This was a task for both Jews and Christians.

But, now, if this is the place of psychoanalysis in the history of civilization—at least, according to Freud—consider its commitments. The entire being of psychoanalysis is now understood as the best response yet to an actual act of aggression. This interpretation implies, first, that the central task of psychoanalysis is the acknowledgment of guilt.

Second, although there may be all sorts of guilty fantasies to analyze, and there will be room for analysis of the superego and so on, at bottom there is a fundamental act of aggression which must lie outside the analysis. The primal crime itself—the killing of the primal father—is unanalyzable because Freud treats it as an actual event rather than a fantasy—an event which inaugurates history and mindedness as we know it. Thus one can analyze the various fantastic responses to this act of aggression, but one cannot analyze the aggression itself. And, remember, this act is supposed to have left a trace in all of us which we pass on to our children as part of our "phylogenetic inheritance." This would seem to suggest that there is a surd element of guilt in all of us that simply cannot be reached by psychoanalysis. Now according to Freud, the actual killing of Moses reawakened in the Hebrew people the memory of the primal crime—to traumatic effect. But, given Freud's structure, one cannot even consider a reverse possibility: that a fantasy of primal crime played a role in the Hebrew people's acting out their aggression. Nor can one consider the possibility that both events are fantasies (one of them being Freud's). Thus the effect of Freud's proposal is to remove material from the domain of psychoanalytic consideration.

What a confining vision! This is at once a metaphysics of aggression and a metaphysics of bad faith. It is a metaphysics of aggression inasmuch as the basic acts of aggression are taken to be part of the fundamental order of our universe. They lie outside the scope of analysis, though they serve to define the field of psychological responses which analysis can address. And it is a metaphysics of bad faith inasmuch as it declares that we are inevitably victims of unjustified guilt. We necessarily bear the guilt of a crime we did not commit. The archaic trace we bear within us—that is, Freud's fantasy of there being such a trace—is the concrete expression of bad faith.

Consider how much opens up if we simply break with this picture. First, there should be no presumption that guilt is the fundamental legacy that civilization bequeaths to our souls. If one sees civilization as itself on a developmental path that runs Judaism, Christianity, psychoanalysis . . . , then one will of course see psychoanalysis as inheriting the problems of its forebears. But this is what it is for psychoanalysis to get trapped in an oedipal fantasy of its own—a family romance, if you will. If Judaism is the father and Christianity the mother, how can I find my place? The right response is not—as Freud did—to try to answer this question, but to break with the fantasy that prompts it. Give up the fantasy that civilization has a developmental structure. And give up the fantasy that we will really understand what psychoanalysis is when we understand its place in that structure. We are then open to the possibility that psychoanalysis is not part of any developmental unfolding, but itself represents a break that opens up new possibilities. Certainly, there should no longer be a presumption when we begin an analysis that guilt is what we shall find, and guilt is what we must treat. That would be our fate if psychoanalysis really were a souped-up version of Christianity. Psychoanalytic freedom begins when we give up that fantasy.

Second, if we abandon the metaphysics of aggression we can at last begin to study aggression from a properly psychoanalytic point of view. Breaking with metaphysical fantasy itself involves two steps. (1) Abandon the aggressive version of the seduction theory. The primal crime is an important fantasy, not an actual event. As such, we can analyze it rather than bow down before it. Doing this is not to turn our backs on real-life aggression and its effects. Quite the contrary. If we stop treating a fantasy of aggression as an actual historical event, we become open to treating real-life aggressions in a more realistic way. (2) Abandon the notion of the aggressive drive (at least for now). We can accept the obvious—namely, that aggression is a fundamental problem for humans, both as individuals and socially—without committing the fallacy of assuming that *therefore* there must be a fundamental force which expresses it. At this point in our research, we cannot do anything with the "aggressive drive" except introduce it into theory as another enigmatic signifier. We might then indulge in the fantasy that we have explained something—that we have finally faced up to the problem of aggression by dealing with the

aggressive drive and its derivatives. All we have really done is inhibit genuine psychoanalytic investigation with a fantasy of having
already found what we are looking for. At some point, there may
be reason to posit an aggressive drive: if, for instance, we could
chart its vicissitudes in the same kind of detail that Freud did for
the sexual drive. Until then, we open up the field of psychoanalytic possibilities if we recognize that the "aggressive drive" is an
ersatz principle.

I have been arguing that if we are to take a step forward in a psychoanalytic understanding of aggression we have to be aggressive
with its metaphysics. It seems fitting, then, to conclude with a
psychoanalytic critique of the fundamental metaphysical image of
Western philosophy. It is, as we shall see, philosophy's metaphysics of aggression. So, let us leave Jerusalem and go back to
Athens, where we began these lectures. (Freud was, of course,
fascinated with both the Judaic and the Hellenic influences on
Western civilization, and this back-and-forth trip is one he made
many times.)

In response to Athenian aggression against Socrates, Plato introduced this enigmatic image into philosophy:

Imagine human beings living in an underground, cave-
like dwelling, with an entrance a long way up, which is
both open to the light and as wide as the cave itself.
They've been there since childhood, fixed in the same
place, with their necks and legs fettered, able to see only
in front of them, because their bonds prevent them from

turning their heads around. Light is provided by a fire burning far above and behind them. Also behind them, but on higher ground, there is a path stretching between them and the fire. Imagine that along this path a low wall has been built, like the screen in front of puppeteers above which they show their puppets.

I'm imagining it.

Then imagine that there are people along the wall, carrying all kinds of artifacts that project above it—statues of people and other animals, made out of stone, wood and every material. And, as you'd expect, some of the carriers are talking, and some are silent.

It's an enigmatic image you're describing, and enigmatic prisoners.

They're like us. Do you suppose, first of all, that these prisoners see anything of themselves and one another besides the shadows that the fire casts on the wall in front of them? (*Republic* VII.514a–515a; my emphasis)[37]

The manifest content of this metaphor is that there is a difference between the manifest content and latent content of our experience. "The prisoners would in every way believe that the truth is nothing other than the shadows of those artifacts" (515c). Plato's account of the prisoner who is initially freed from his bonds must have been an inspiration for Freud's own account of resistance in analytic therapy. When the prisoner first turned around, he would feel pain and be dazzled by the light. "And if someone dragged him away from there by force, up the rough, steep path, and didn't let him go until he had dragged him into the sunlight, wouldn't he be pained and irritated at being treated that way? And when he came into the light with the sun filling his eyes, wouldn't he be unable to see a single one of the things now said to be true?" (515e–516a). The ascent requires habituation, getting used to the light, getting used to seeing things directly rather than their distorted appearances. But if one stuck with the arduous ascent, one would finally "be able to see the sun, not images of it in water or some alien place, but the sun itself, in its own place and be able to study it. And at this point he would infer and conclude that the sun . . . governs everything in the visible world, and is in some way the cause of all the things that he used to see" (516b–c).

Although Plato's picture is darker and more radical than Aristotle's cheerful and normalized view of ethics, they have the same basic structure. For both thinkers, ethical life within culture defines a structure which, within that context, makes claims to happiness but which, by the very setting up of that structure, establishes an outside—a place that it is almost impossible to reach—in which *true* happiness can be found. For both thinkers, in that outside position one engages in an impractical activity: contemplation of the cause of all things. In the best life, then, one leaves the mother's breast and engages in an arduous journey by which one eventually "returns" to the metaphysical breast, the source of all things.

It is this gap between wisdom and what passes for such in the ordinary world that, for Plato, explains the death of Socrates. For if someone who had seen the form of the good returned to the cave, his eyes would be "filled with darkness":

And before his eyes had recovered—and the adjustment would not be quick—while his vision was still dim, if he had to compete again with the perpetual prisoners in recognizing the shadows, wouldn't he invite ridicule? Wouldn't it be said of him that he'd returned from his upward journey with his eyesight ruined and that it isn't worthwhile even to try to travel upward? And, as for anyone who tried to free them and lead them upward, if they could somehow get their hands on him, wouldn't they kill him? (516e–517a)

The response of the interlocutor: "They certainly would." So one purpose of this metaphor is to make explicable an otherwise puzzling event—a supposedly advanced culture putting to death by democratic vote the best man among them. Indeed, this account of our metaphysics situation makes Socrates' death look inevitable. This, then, is the manifest image of the cave.

What does it cover over? Surely, there is an attempt here to contain human aggression within the overall confines of the good. Everything distorted is contained within the cave. Outside is the sun, the form of the good. Inside the cave, people are unconsciously trapped inside distorting fantasies, but all the distortions are distortions of a higher reality. The prisoners are watching shadows, but those shadows are projected from the light of a fire—itself an imitation of the light of the sun—onto cultural artifacts being paraded *higher up* in the cave. I take it that Plato is referring to Homer, Hesiod, Pindar, and the other great poets who shaped Greek culture by providing (what Plato took to be) a fundamentally misleading picture of the gods and their relations with humans. Still, Plato places them higher up: they are straining toward a glimpse of the divine, even if they themselves have distorted visions.

This picture is meant to be ontologically exhaustive: existence inside and outside the cave gives us all the possibilities there are. This image appears unlimited because it gives us its own account of limitation. To mistake a restricted field of possibilities for all the possibilities there are is, *on this image,* precisely what it is to be an inhabitant of the cave. It thereby becomes extremely difficult to imagine that the entire metaphor of the cave—outside as well as inside—is one more constrained vision of the field of possibilities.

Inside the cave it is possible for people to behave badly. But in this way the phenomenon of human badness is explained and contained within the overall framework of the good. There may be fallings away from the good, there may be distortions of the good, but that is all that badness can be. There is no doubt but that Western metaphysics has been dominated by this image.

Within this conception, the only discontent recognized is in relation to the good. We feel pain and discomfort when we are turned toward the sun and make our ascent; we again feel discomfort on our return descent; we also feel discomfort if we have not made any ascent, but someone who has comes into our midst. On this picture, it is the good that shakes us up. Of course, the inhabitants of the cave will put a Socrates figure to death; but that is because their own (fantastically distorted) orientation to the good is being disturbed. In their own misguided attempts to live a good life, they mistake "Socrates" as a force for bad. And thus they understand their attack upon him as an attempt to preserve the good. And although Plato thinks they are gravely mistaken about what they actually are doing, in fact he agrees with them about their motivation. Their motivation *is* for the good, albeit in wildly distorted form. There is no room in the metaphor of the cave for an attack on the good that is motivated as such. One might say that in the cave there is room for jealousy, but no room for envy.

In a funny way, this could have been Freud's metaphor up until the moment that he wrote *Beyond the Pleasure Principle.* For up until that point, unconscious mental processes were wishful fantasies directed along paths of the loose associations of primary process toward some distorted image of a good. But from the perspective of *Beyond the Pleasure Principle,* the metaphor of the cave gives a false picture of the totality of human possibilities. Given the whole structure of the cave, with its fantasies and distortions, there is some further disruptive force that breaks up this structure. This source of disruption necessarily cannot be understood in terms of a desire for the good, no matter how distorted. And thus it cannot be a fantasy in the Platonic sense. There is no place inside or outside the cave for this disruptive force. The cave cannot contain this force—and thus this force is disruptive of the metaphor itself. The metaphor of the cave is meant to contain its own outside within itself: outside the cave is the sun, the form of the good. What *Beyond the Pleasure Principle* introduces is, as it were, the need for an outside to this outside. I say "as it were" because by now it should be clear that we do not need another place—even in a metaphor.

What we need to grasp is not another place but a peculiar kind of possibility: the possibility of disrupting the field of possibilities. This possibility seems almost paradoxical, since in any attempt to describe the field of possibilities, it gets left out. It is precisely that which disrupts the field, and thus is experienced as coming from "outside" or "beyond." Ironically, when it comes to human living, the field of possibilities is not a field. Or, to put it less paradoxically: any purported field of possibilities is always a somewhat restricting fantasy of what is possible in human life.

We are now in a position to see what a deep rejection psychoanalysis offers of the teleological understanding of human being. One sees this in part by contrasting it with Plato's and Aristotle's attempts to contain human life within the teleological, even as they feel it breaking out. For Plato and for Aristotle, there are, importantly, two levels of teleological commitment. The first level is obvious and familiar: human desire is toward the good; conflicts, irrationality, and badness are to be explained in terms of conflicts among desires, fantasies, distortions, ignorance, and bad upbringing. On this conception, irrationality and unconscious motivation could be included as an extension of folk psychology. Both thinkers recognize that ethical life—whether the ordinary ethical life of Athenian culture or the virtuous ethical life that Aristotle characterizes—sets up an outside. And—this is the second level of teleological commitment—both thinkers try to contain this outside within the teleological framework. "Outside" for Plato is the sun; "outside" for Aristotle is contemplation. Both thinkers want to give the outside a name, and the name is "good." Both thinkers want to give a name to what it would be to get there: "happiness."

The first level of teleological commitment looks plausible enough in its own terms (even if it is ultimately inadequate), but, from a psychoanalytic point of view, this second level of commitment begins to look a bit desperate. After all, if the *real* good lies just outside the established ethical system, why not aim to get there directly? This question arises most obviously for Aristotle. Why did Aristotle spend the first ninety-seven percent of the *Nicomachean Ethics* justifying and explaining the ethically virtuous life, only, in the last few pages, to turn us obliquely to a different good?[38] Of course, there may be many reasons for this—for example, that, rhetorically, it is the best way to bring his audience along. But such a claim makes it look as though the issue is a matter of argumentative taste—that is, as though it were a contingent matter. The psychoanalytic point is that the issue is not really contemplation, but a constitutive fantasy of "outside." Once Aristotle has constructed an image of the ethical life, he feels pressure to construct a picture of what lies beyond. And what he is trying to do is to contain that "beyond" within the teleological. In my view, it is yet another fantasy to think that if only Aristotle had included contemplation prominently and up front in the *Ethics,* he could have written a unified ethical account that could have captured life without remainder. Writing such a book would itself have put internal pressure on Aristotle to come up with an image of what lies outside. Of course, he might have ignored that pressure or pretended he had somehow accounted for it—but it would be there nonetheless. The beauty of the route Aristotle did take is that it enabled him both to construct a satisfying picture of ethical life and to capture the "beyond" that remained inside his overall teleological outlook.

On the surface, it looks as though Plato has given us an empirical explanation for why humans cannot get to the good directly: they are trapped by fantasies that captivate and mislead them. And, of course, from a psychoanalytic perspective this empirical explanation is true: humans do tend to be ensnared in lives dominated by unconscious fantasies. But there is a further psychoanalytic point: although it may be true that humans are trapped in unconscious fantasies, this is not the reason they cannot get to the good directly. Rather, it is constitutive of human life—life influenced by fantasy, life in society, ethical life—that there is an experience that there is something more to life, something left out. There is an inchoate sense that there is a remainder to life, something that is not captured in life as it is so far experienced. Thus there is pressure to construct an image of what lies outside.

Plato's fantasy of outside actually gives us a glimpse of what is so dangerous about it. For the idea is that ordinary life, restricted as it is by fantasy, is necessarily limited, but that if only we could break through all these limitations we would arrive at absolute knowledge and absolute happiness. And the suggestion of the fantasy is not that this realm of absolute happiness is totally shut off from humans—for example, available only to the gods—but that on some rare occasion some lucky bugger can get through. In Plato's view, Socrates was just that lucky bugger. He broke through the restrictions of ordinary life and was able to achieve absolute happiness—*that's* why the Athenians killed him. At least, according to Plato's fantasy. Now what is interesting is that something like this may have also been the fantasy of the

Athenian citizens who voted for Socrates' death. It is not that every Athenian had a fully formed fantasy of the cave. But there was an inchoate sense that life is restricted, that there is an out-side—and that somehow Socrates managed to get there. The only way to get him back inside the confines of Athenian law was to kill him.

In this interpretation, Plato was mistaken about what he was doing. He was not, in fact, offering a metaphor of ultimate meta-physical reality; he was offering an interpretation of the fantasies of those who killed Socrates. And if the fantasy of an outside is constitutive of ethical life, we can see why the image of the cave has had such a powerful influence. For it is an image which struc-tures the inchoate fantasies of those who are already living within the ethical.

I have been arguing that the *latent* content of the metaphor of the cave is that human aggression could be contained within an overall framework of the good. One of the fundamental moments in the development of psychoanalysis comes with Freud's recog-nition that this is not possible. But instead of abandoning the metaphor of the cave altogether, Freud comes up with a variant. Inside the cave is the world of human striving: humans are domi-nated by unconscious fantasies that distort their vision of reality and inhibit their lives. Analysis provides a means of ascent, through massive resistance, toward a kind of truthfulness. But to locate this world *inside* a cave, one needs an outside—and this Freud supplies with his enigmatic signifier, "death."

This whole theoretical structure is only one more instance of the cave, and if psychoanalysis has taught us anything, it is that the wealth of human possibilities cannot be contained by any variant of this image. To live with human possibility, one has to tolerate a peculiar kind of theoretical anxiety: the willingness to live without a principle. Only then can we begin to grasp the peculiar possibility for possibilities that human being opens up.

NOTES

ONE / HAPPINESS

1. See John McDowell, "Virtue and Reason," in *Mind, Value, and Reality* (Cambridge, Mass.: Harvard University Press, 1998).

2. We owe to Jacques Lacan and Jean Laplanche the idea that the history of psychoanalysis can be read as a history of the resistance to its own insight. See Jean Laplanche, *Life and Death in Psychoanalysis* (Baltimore: Johns Hopkins University Press, 1985); idem, "The Unfinished Copernican Revolution," in *Essays on Otherness* (London: Routledge, 1999); and Jacques Lacan, *The Ego in Freud's Theory and In the Technique of Psychoanalysis, 1954–1955* (New York: W. W. Norton, 1988); idem, *Freud's Papers on Technique, 1953–1954* (New York: W. W. Norton, 1988).

3. See, for example, Bernard Williams, *Ethics and the Limits of Philosophy* (Cambridge, Mass.: Harvard University Press, 1985).

4. Interestingly, Freud seems blind to the ways in which the Aristotelian approach to the virtues was itself taken up in the Christian tradition.

5. I also have a personal reason for going back to Aristotle. My time in Cambridge—which stretched out over fifteen years—was one of the great personal and intellectual experiences of my life. It has certainly influenced everything I've done since. For much of that time my studying and teaching were absorbed in a philosophical engagement with Aristotle. When I left Cambridge, I trained as a psychoanalyst, and when I wanted to read or teach a Greek philosopher, I turned to Plato. Now, returning to Cambridge fourteen years later, I am fascinated by the question of what it would be, for me, to return to Aristotle. For me to see how my reading of him would now differ from my earlier readings would be to take a measure of how I have changed—of what difference psychoanalysis has made to me. Perhaps I should note in passing that when I first came to Cambridge there was no Philosophy Tripos. One read the Moral Sciences. What's in a name? As we shall see: a lot and nothing. A lesson that emerges from these lectures is that psychoanalysis could never be included in the Moral Sciences—except as a limiting case, as that which disrupts the moral sciences—whereas it could be included as a peculiar kind of mental activity that was properly called philosophical.

6. Aristotle, *Ethica Nicomachea* (Oxford: Clarendon Press, 1975; hereafter cited as *EN*), I.1.1094a1–3; my emphasis. English translations, unless otherwise noted, are from *The Complete Works of Aristotle: The Revised Oxford*, trans. L. W. D. Ross and J. O. Urmson (Princeton: Princeton University Press, 1984).

7. See Sarah Broadie, *Ethics with Aristotle* (Oxford: Oxford University Press, 1991), p. 9.

8. Ludwig Wittgenstein, *Philosophical Investigations*, trans. G. E. M. Anscombe (Oxford: Basil Blackwell, 1978), I.185–189.

9. Lacan, *The Ego in Freud's Theory*, pp. 15–21, 256–257. See also S. G. Shanker, *Wittgenstein and the Turning Point in the Philosophy of Mathematics* (Albany: State University of New York Press, 1987).

10. *EN* I.2.1094a22–25.

11. *EN* I.1.1094a4–18.

12. *EN* I.2.1094a18–22.

13. *EN* I.4.1094b27–1095a11; 1095b2–13.

14. *EN* I.3.1095a10–11.

15. *EN* I.2.1094a22–b11.

16. See Broadie, *Ethics with Aristotle,* pp. 15–16.

17. See Plato, *Gorgias* 515–521.

18. Philip Roth, *Portnoy's Complaint* (New York: Random House, 1967).

19. *EN* X.9.1181b12–23.

20. *EN* I.4.1095a14; I.5.1095b14; I.7.1097a15, a25.

21. I do not want to hang anything in the argument on this, but one might note in passing that it is precisely here that Aristotle launches an explicit attack on his philosophical father: "We had better consider the universal good and discuss thoroughly what is meant by it, although such an inquiry is made an uphill one by the fact that the Forms have been introduced by friends of our own. Yet it would perhaps be thought to be better, indeed to be our duty, for the sake of maintaining the truth even to destroy what touches us closely, especially as we are philosophers; for while both are dear, piety requires us to honor truth above our friends" (*EN* I.6.1096a11–16). One might wonder: why the need to appeal to truth and piety to justify an aggressive attack?

22. *EN* I.4.1095a14–30; my emphasis.

23. See, for example, *Studies on Hysteria,* in *The Standard Edition of the Complete Psychological Works of Sigmund Freud,* ed. and trans. James E. Strachey (London: Hogarth Press, 1981; cited hereafter as *SE*), vol. 2.

24. Most notably Laplanche, *Life and Death in Psychoanalysis* and "The Unfinished Copernican Revolution." Compare Hans Loewald,

"Primary Process, Secondary Process and Language," in *Papers on Psychoanalysis* (New Haven: Yale University Press: 1980), pp. 184–191.

25. I discuss this interpretation of the seduction hypothesis in *Open Minded: Working Out the Logic of the Soul* (Cambridge, Mass.: Harvard University Press, 1998), chap. 2.

26. See, for example, the account of Solon's visit to Croesus in Herodotus, *The Histories*, trans. Aubrey de Selincourt (New York: Penguin Books, 1972), bk. I.

27. *EN* I.7.1097a18–23.

28. *EN* I.7.1097a25–34.

29. *EN* I.7.1097b5–17.

30. I owe this happy turn of phrase to Gabriel Richardson.

31. *EN* I.7.1097b22–25.

32. *EN* I.7.1098a3–17.

33. *EN* I.9.1099b32–1100a1.

34. *EN* I.7.1098a18–20.

35. See *EN* I.10.

36. *EN* I.10.1100a34–b1.

37. *EN* I.11.1101a22–b9.

38. *EN* I.8.1098b9–12.

39. *EN* I.8.1098b20–22.

40. *EN* I.8–9.1098b30–1099b17.

41. In this context, note the way that Plato chooses to end the *Symposium*: "At that point, Aristodemus said, Eryximachus, Phaedrus, and some others among the original guests made their excuses and left. He himself fell asleep and slept for a long time (it was winter, and the nights were quite long). He woke up just as dawn was about to break; the roosters were crowing already. He saw that the others had either left or were asleep on their couches and that only Agathon, Aristophanes, and Socrates were still awake, drinking out of a large cup which they were

passing around from left to right. Socrates was talking to them. Aristo-demus couldn't remember exactly what they were saying—*he'd missed the first part of their discussion, and he was half-asleep anyway—but the main point was that Socrates was trying to prove to them that authors should be able to write both comedy and tragedy: the skillful tragic dramatist should also be a comic poet. He was about to clinch his argument,* though to tell the truth, sleepy as they were, they were hardly able to follow his reasoning. In fact, Aristophanes fell asleep in the middle of the discussion, and very soon thereafter, as day was breaking, Agathon also drifted off"; Plato, *Symposium,* trans. Alexander Nehamas and Paul Woodruff (Indianapolis: Hackett, 1989), 223b–d.

In other words, Socrates dramatizes a scene in which there is nothing left but an enigmatic message. Everyone has left or fallen asleep, there is no one left who can reconstruct the argument—and yet we feel that the message is crucial and somehow matters *to us.* Is there any choice but to create an interpretation? To understand the torrent of writing, thinking, interpretation that this seduction brought forth is to understand much of the history of Western literary criticism.

42. I discuss a related point about our mindedness in "Transcendental Anthropology," in *Open Minded.*

43. *EN* I.9.1099b33–1100a1; see also X.8.1178b24–25.

44. *EN* X.8.1178a9.

45. See, e.g., *EN* I.5.1095b14–1096a5; I.9.1099b11–18; I.12.1101-b21–31.

46. See Broadie, *Ethics with Aristotle,* pp. 26–27, on the central good.

47. *EN* X.7.1177a12–18.

48. *EN* X.7.1177a27–b26; my emphasis.

49. *EN* X.8.1178a9–b22; my emphasis.

50. See Freud, *Project for a Scientific Psychology, SE* 1: 350–359;

Laplanche, *Life and Death in Psychoanalysis*, chap. 2; and Jean Laplanche and J.-B. Pontalis, "Deferred Action," in *The Language of Psychoanalysis* (London: Hogarth Press, 1983), pp. 111–114.

51. *EN* X.7.1177b26–1178a8; my emphasis.

52. See also *EN* X.8.1179a22–32: the double-edged message continues.

53. Cf. *EN* X.7.1177b5.

54. See, e.g., *EN* X.8.1178b20 ff.

55. *EN* X.8.1178b24.

56. *EN* X.9.1179a34–b2.

57. *EN* X.9.1179b10–1180a5.

58. *EN* X.9.1180a1–5.

59. *EN* X.9.1180a14–24; my emphasis.

60. *EN* X.9.1181b12–23, 1180b23–1181a14, 1180a24–32.

TWO / DEATH

1. *NE* III.7.1115b17–20.

2. *NE* I.10.

3. Freud, *Beyond the Pleasure Principle, SE* 18: 13; my emphasis.

4. Ibid., p. 13; my emphasis.

5. For more detailed accounts, see Freud, *Project for a Scientific Psychology, SE* 1: 295–345; Jacques Lacan, *The Seminar of Jacques Lacan, Book II: The Ego in Freud's Theory and in the Technique of Psychoanalysis, 1954–1955* (Cambridge: Cambridge University Press, 1988), pp. 27–145; John Friedman, *The Origins of Self and Identity: Living and Dying in Freud's Psychoanalysis* (Northvale, N. J.: Jason Aronson, 1998), pp. 41–70; Jean Laplanche, *Life and Death in Psychoanalysis* (Baltimore: Johns Hopkins University Press, 1985), pp. 48–84.

6. If we interpret Aristotle's valuation of contemplation in these

Freudian terms, contemplation is the maximal way of mentally diffusing tension as, in its ultimate form, it is a way of seeing and thinking how *everything* fits together.

7. Freud, *Beyond the Pleasure Principle, SE* 18: 29-30.

8. Ibid., p. 32; my emphasis.

9. Ibid., pp. 32–33; my emphasis.

10. Ibid., p. 22.

11. Ibid., p. 62.

12. Ibid., p. 21; my emphasis.

13. Ibid., p. 23.

14. Ibid., p. 32; my emphasis. See also the account of trauma quoted on page 71 above. On this account there is first a disruption and only subsequently an attempt to "bind" the excitation by providing a content. See also pp. 34–35, where Freud says: "it would be the task of the higher strata of the mental apparatus to bind the instinctual excitation reaching the primary process. A failure to effect this binding would provoke a disturbance analogous to a traumatic neurosis; and only after the binding has been accomplished would it be possible for the dominance of the pleasure principle (and of its modification, the reality principle) to proceed unhindered." See also Freud's essay "The Loss of Reality in Neurosis and Psychosis," in which he argues that psychotic fantasy is, in effect, an attempt at healing, an attempt to heal over a nameless breach (*SE* 19: 183–187).

15. I began to use the analogy with Darwin to illuminate Freud's theory of mental functioning in *Open Minded: Working Out the Logic of the Soul* (Cambridge, Mass.: Harvard University Press, 1998), pp. 121–122.

16. It is almost, but not quite, needless to say that this striving is neither intentional nor conscious. The striving is to be understood in terms of goal-directed activity.

17. Freud, *Beyond the Pleasure Principle, SE* 18: 36. Throughout this essay I use the word "drive" for *Trieb,* which in the *Standard Edition* is translated as "instinct." See Laplanche, *Life and Death in Psychoanalysis,* chap. 1.

18. This can be difficult for us to grasp because even the most brutal repetitions of the traumatic neuroses can acquire a function. So, for instance, a repetitive traumatic dream can trigger anxiety and can then acquire a signal function, bringing anxiety about. There is no doubt that many eruptions in the mind can acquire functions in this way. This is an analogue of how a random eruption in nature can get selected. Also, if we treat all repetitions as forming a unified class then we will, of course, tend to assume that repetitions must have a function. For the repetitions of children's games, habits, neurotic repetitions, cultural rituals, and so on obviously have purposes. The point though is not that repetitions can have or acquire purposes, but whether each and every repetition must itself be explained as the product of an elementary force that itself has a purpose.

19. Freud, *Beyond the Pleasure Principle, SE* 18: 37–38; my emphasis.

20. Although I am in general skeptical of attempts to speculate about a person on the basis of his published work, I will give in to the temptation to say that I suspect that Freud is here caught up in a fantasy of self-realization. In *The Interpretation of Dreams* we learn that when Freud was a boy he one night urinated in the parental bedroom and his father said to his mother in exasperation, "The boy will come to nothing." Even in adult life, Freud finds in the analysis of his dreams an enduring wishful fantasy to respond to his father, "You see, I have come to something" (*SE* 4: 216, 169–176, 106–121; 5: 421–425). In terms of the current discussion, the paternal utterance functions for Freud as an enigmatic signifier. He knows the utterance has a special

meaning for him—it is oracular—but he doesn't quite understand what it means. His life takes on the shape of one who wishes to prove the oracle wrong. The invention/discovery of psychoanalysis, the science of oracles, is Freud's own way of responding to his enigmatic signifier.

21. See, for example, Jacques Lacan, *The Ethics of Psychoanalysis 1959–1960: The Seminar of Jacques Lacan Book VII* (New York: W. W. Norton, 1992), pp. 115–127, 139–154, 167–178, 191–217, 270–287.

22. Freud, *Beyond the Pleasure Principle, SE* 18: 63.

23. See, e.g., ibid., pp. 53–55; Freud, *Civilization and Its Discontents, SE* 21: 118–121. On reflection it is clear that Freud must have recourse to the concept of repetition if he is to link all the otherwise disparate phenomena under the death drive. For at first he invokes the death drive to account for disruptions of mental functioning—e.g., those eruptions of traumatic neurosis that put the pleasure principle out of action. But later he sees the pleasure principle itself as functioning in accordance with the death drive. How can one bring together such apparent opposites under one concept? It is clear that, for Freud, "repetition" is functioning as the essential middle term. The repeated breaks in the functioning of the pleasure principle are manifestations of the repetition compulsion—and the established forms of mental functioning (whether by pleasure principle or reality principle) are forms of repetition. If the concept of repetition did not play a central role, there would be no way to unite these otherwise distinct phenomena.

24. Freud, *Civilization and Its Discontents, SE* 21: 120.

25. Hanna Segal, *Introduction to the Work of Melanie Klein* (New York: Basic Books, 1979); R. D. Hinshelwood, *Clinical Klein* (London: Free Association Books, 1994); Melanie Klein, *Envy and Gratitude and Other Works, 1946–1963* (London: Virago Press, 1988); Wilfrid Bion, "At-

tacks on Linking" in *Melanie Klein Today: Developments in Theory and Practice*, vol. 1: *Mainly Practice*, ed. E. B. Spillius (New York: Routledge 1988); D. W. Winnicott, *Through Paediatrics to Psycho-Analysis* (London: Hogarth Press, 1982); Paul Gray, The *Ego and the Analysis of Defense* (Northvale, N. J.: Jason Aronson, 1994); Marianne Goldberger, ed., *Danger and Defense: The Technique of Close Process Attention* (Northvale, N. J.: Jason Aronson, 1996).

26. See Freud, *Beyond the Pleasure Principle, SE* 18: 23.

27. Ibid., pp. 14–15; my emphases.

28. See Bion, "Attacks on Linking."

29. In a footnote, Freud observes that at the same time the child invents a game of making himself disappear; *Beyond the Pleasure Principle, SE* 18: 15n. There is a fascinating discussion of this in Friedman, *The Origins of Self and Identity*, pp. 122–123.

30. *EN* X.7.1177.

31. Plato, *Republic* 3.368d–e, 4.434d.

32. Plato, *Apology*.

33. In this light it is worth rereading the *Charmides,* in which it becomes clear not merely that no one can say what temperance is, but that no one really knows how to think about the question. The dialogue is directed less to saying what temperance is than to trying to figure out ways to think about the question.

34. See, for example, Alcibiades' description at Plato, *Symposium* 221c–d.

35. See Søren Kierkegaard, *The Concept of Irony with Continual Reference to Socrates,* trans. Howard V. Horg (Princeton: Princeton University Press, 1989).

36. Plato, *Symposium,* e.g., 215d–e, 172b–173d, 174b, 213c, 222e–223b.

37. And according to Plato's myth of recollection, what the philos-

opher is striving for is something he once had (before birth) but lost. On this myth, philosophy is an attempt to regain the lost object.

THREE / THE REMAINDER OF LIFE

1. See Jacques Lacan, *The Ethics of Psychoanalysis, 1959–1960* (New York: W. W. Norton), pp. 43–70. His discussion of "The Thing" is one version of this fantasy.

2. Sigmund Freud, "Analysis Terminable and Interminable," *SE* 23: 226–227.

3. Ibid., p. 226; my emphasis.

4. Ibid., pp. 229–230; my emphasis.

5. This is well described in John A. Friedman, *The Origins of Self and Identity: Living and Dying in Freud's Psychoanalysis* (Northvale, N. J.: Jason Aronson, 1998). See especially chap. 4, "Freud's *Todestrieb*." It is also one part of Lacan's understanding of the death drive. See *The Ethics of Psychoanalysis,* pp. 35–42, 205–217.

6. Freud, "On Narcissism: An Introduction," *SE* 14: 85; my emphasis.

7. See Wilfrid Bion, "Attacks on Linking," in *Melanie Klein Today: Developments in Theory and Practice,* vol. 1: *Mainly Practice,* ed. E. B. Spillins (New York: Routledge, 1988).

8. See Harold Bloom, *Anxiety of Influence: A Theory of Poetry* (New York: Oxford University Press, 1973); Hans Loewald, "The Waning of the Oedipus Complex," in *Papers on Psychoanalysis* (New Haven: Yale University Press, 1980).

9. This is a central theme of Lacan's *Ethics of Psychoanalysis.*

10. I discuss at length the idea that in the transference the analysand creates an idiosyncratic polis—an *idiopolis*—in "An Interpretation of

Transference," in *Open Minded: Working Out the Logic of the Soul* (Cambridge, Mass.: Harvard University Press, 1998), chap. 4.

11. See Hanna Segal, *Introduction to the Work of Melanie Klein* (New York: Basic Books, 1979); R. D. Hinschelwood, *Clinical Klein* (London: Free Association Books, 1994); Melanie Klein, "Notes on Some Schizoid Mechanisms," in *Developments in Psycho-analysis,* ed. M. Klein, S. Isaacs, and J. Riviere (London: Hogarth Press, 1970).

12. I discuss the interpretation of this moment at some length in "Restlessness, Phantasy, and the Concept of Mind" in *Open Minded.*

13. Freud, *Notes on a Case of Obsessional Neurosis, SE* 10: 209.

14. This insight has been mined deeply by Donald Davidson. See *Inquiries into Truth and Interpretation* (Oxford: Clarendon Press, 1984). In the specific case of unconscious beliefs, see his essay "Paradoxes of Irrationality" in *Philosophical Essays on Freud,* ed. R. Wollheim and J. Hopkins (Cambridge: Cambridge University Press, 1982). I offer a critique of this interpretation of the unconscious in "Restlessness, Phantasy, and the Concept of Mind."

15. See Brian Bird, "Notes on Transference: Universal Phenomenon and Hardest Part of Analysis," *Journal of the American Psychoanalytic Association* 20 (1972): 267–301.

16. At the time I was struck by an uncanny resemblance to an event that Freud describes in *Studies on Hysteria.* At a point in his analysis of Miss Lucy R., Freud discovers and then confronts Miss R. with the fact that she is in love with her boss. "She answered in her usual laconic fashion: 'Yes, I think that's true.'—'But if you knew you loved your employer why didn't you tell me?'—'I didn't know—or rather I didn't want to know. I wanted to drive it out of my head and not think of it again; and I believe latterly that I have succeeded.'" In a footnote Freud comments: "I have never managed to give a better description than this of the strange state of mind in which one knows and does not know a

thing at the same time. It is clearly impossible to understand it unless one has been in such a state oneself"; *SE* 2: 117.

17. See John McDowell, "Virtue and Reason" in *Mind, Value, and Reality* (Cambridge, Mass.: Harvard University Press, 1998), pp. 50–74.

18. See Freud, "Analysis Terminable and Interminable," *SE* 23: 219–220.

19. Freud, *Civilization and Its Discontents, SE* 21: 120.

20. Ibid., p. 119.

21. Ibid., pp. 125–126, 128, 129.

22. Ibid., p. 119.

23. Ibid.; my emphasis.

24. Of course, if we stick with strictly Freudian terminology, there is a sense in which Freud does not treat the death drive as a principle either. For he seems to distinguish principles of mental functioning—the pleasure principle and the reality principle—from drives such as the sexual drive and the death drive. Although Freud is somewhat unclear—and perhaps equivocal—in general, drives are characteristic forces within the system which operate according to principles. So, to take a paradigmatic example, the sexual drive operates according to the pleasure principle. The issue becomes problematic with the death drive, which Freud seems to treat sometimes as a drive, sometimes as a principle. However that may be, I am using the term "principle" in a general and colloquial sense, so that Freud's sexual drive and death drive, insofar as they are forces for directed strivings, would count as principles.

25. Freud, *Civilization and Its Discontents, SE* 21: 119.

26. Ibid., p. 86.

27. See Robert A. Paul, *Moses and Civilization: The Meaning behind Freud's Myth* (New Haven: Yale University Press, 1996).

28. Freud, *Civilization and Its Discontents, SE* 21: 76.

29. See Jean-Pierre Vernant and Pierre Vidal-Naquet, *Myth and Tragedy in Ancient Greece* (New York: Zone Books, 1990), p. 27.

30. Freud, *Civilization and Its Discontents, SE* 21: 74.

31. For the most fascinating account of the myth of the primal father as an organizing myth (as opposed to actual event), see Paul, *Moses and Civilization.*

32. Freud, *Moses and Monotheism, SE* 23: 88–90; my emphases.

33. Ibid., pp. 88–90; my emphases.

34. Of course, one can say that at some level the seduction hypothesis keeps coming back for me. For the manifest content of the sophisticated version of the seduction hypothesis holds that we are necessarily susceptible to enigmatic signifiers. It is to this version alone that I adhere.

35. See Paul, *Moses and Civilization,* which works this out in the case of Judaism and the Torah. The same argument can be made with respect to the primal father: Freud overlooks the possibility that it is a current fantasy, not a historical event, but he deduces it solely from the phenomena of totemism, Christian religion's death of the son to atone for our sins, and Catholic communion.

36. Indeed, Freud explicitly suppresses one of the most important clinical distinctions in psychoanalysis, the difference between a traumatic neurosis and a hysterical neurosis:

"We may leave on one side the question of whether the aetiology of the neuroses in general may be regarded as traumatic. The obvious objection to this is that it is not possible in every case to discover a manifest trauma in the neurotic subject's earliest history. We must often resign ourselves to saying that all we have before us is an unusual, abnormal reaction to experiences and demands which affect everyone, but are worked over and dealt with by other people in another manner which may be called normal. When we have nothing else at our disposal for explaining a neuro-

sis but hereditary and constitutional dispositions, we are naturally tempted to say that it was not acquired but developed.

"But in this connection two points must be stressed. Firstly, the genesis of a neurosis invariably goes back to very early impressions of childhood. Secondly, it is true that there are cases which are distinguished as being 'traumatic' because their effects go back unmistakably to one or more powerful impressions in these early times—impressions which have escaped being dealt with normally, so that one is inclined to judge that if they had not occurred the neurosis would not have come about either. *It would be enough for our purposes if we were obliged to restrict the analogy we are in search of to these traumatic cases.* It is quite possible to unite the two aetiological determinants under a single conception: it is merely a question of how one defines 'traumatic.' If we may assume the experience acquires its traumatic character only as a result of a quantitative factor—that is to say, that in every case it is an excess in demand that is responsible for an experience evoking unusual pathological reactions—then we can easily arrive at the expedient of saying that something acts as a trauma in the case of one constitution but in the case of another would have no such effect . . . *After mentioning this, we can disregard the distinction between traumatic and not-traumatic aetiologies as irrelevant to the analogy we are in search of*" (*Moses and Monotheism, SE* 23: 72–73; my emphases).

This argument does suppress the history of psychoanalysis. In *Studies on Hysteria,* Freud differentiates traumatic neurosis from hysterical neurosis: for traumatic neurosis the precipitating cause is obvious and immediate. Freud argues that hysteria actually has a traumatic *structure,* but that that was not obvious because the originating cause was hidden. He then argued that the hidden cause was a repressed memory, which was currently operating as a direct cause. From this position, Freud was able to move two years later to the idea that the "memory" might instead be a fantasy. This is the moment when the seduction theory is abandoned, and it opens up psychoanalysis to the insight that mind is both imaginative and causal. It is precisely this insight that gets covered over by a collapsing of the distinction between hysterical and traumatic neurosis.

37. With one emendation, the translation is taken from Plato, *Republic,* trans. G. M. A. Grube, rev. C. D. C. Reeve (Indianapolis: Hackett, 1992). The emendation is that for ἄτοπος I use "enigmatic" rather than "strange." This brings the passage into more explicit contact with the concerns of this book. For the Greek text, I have relied on Plato, Πολιτεια, *Platonis Opera* (Oxford: Clarendon Press, 1978).

38. Of course, once the contemplative rabbit has been pulled out of the metaphysical hat, one can see, retrospectively, a few nods and winks in that direction.

ACKNOWLEDGMENTS

I would like to thank all my colleagues at the Committee on Social Thought at the University of Chicago, and especially the current philosopher-king Robert Pippin, for sustaining an environment that promotes independent thought, taking risks, trying things out. My own project has been to try to bring together two disciplines, two loves—philosophy and psychoanalysis—which for contingent reasons have been kept apart. I am particularly grateful to Irad Kimhi, Robert Paul, and Eric Santner, who, in committee seminars and continuing conversations, have taught me much and stimulated me to think. If one is trying to think across disciplines it is hard to know ahead of time from what quarter real stimulation will come. I have found that being able to talk to John Coetzee, a novelist, and Mark Strand, a poet, have been a particular help. Anne Gamboa, the Committee's administrative assistant, has helped me in a thousand ways. Richard Saller, Dean of the Social Sciences, has always supported me in my research.

In my somewhat eccentric life, I commute between Chicago

and New Haven. Tony Dronman, the Dean of the Yale Law School, has given me a library carrel in which to write and has invited me to faculty seminars. It is one of the beauties of that law school that it should welcome such an oddball into its presence. John Davie has saved this book from computer crashes; and Georganne Rogers has saved me from the crashes of work life.

This book was written in response to an invitation to give the Tanner Lectures on Human Values at the University of Cambridge. I should like to thank the members of the Tanner committee, especially its chair, Dame Gillian Beer, the President of Clare Hall. I learned enormously during a daylong seminar from Myles Burnyeat, John Forrester, Sebastian Gardner, Ross Harrison, Mary Jacobus, Juliet Mitchell, and Margot Waddell. Zena Hitz, Ken Gemes, Jane Levin, Richard Levin, Evonne Levy, Gabriel Richardson, and Timothy Smiley provided valuable comments on an earlier draft. Lindsay Waters, the Zenmaster of academic publishing, uttered the koan that allowed me to turn the lectures into a book. Ann Hawthorne at Harvard University Press gave me the line-by-line attention that every author adores. Kimberly Steere was always there with backup support. I am, as ever, aided by the interpretations, patience, and presence of Samuel Ritvo.

If I had not gone to Cambridge about thirty years ago, I would have gone through life under the misapprehension that philosophy was the study of what certain other people had thought. Philosophy as an activity of the soul was brought to life for me by a community of faculty and students who inhabited Cambridge in overlapping parts of the 1970s and 1980s: Elizabeth Anscombe,

ACKNOWLEDGMENTS

Anthony Appiah, Tom Baldwin, Myles Burnyeat, Jeremy Butterfield, Edward Craig, John Dunn, Raymond Geuss, Jane Heal, Sue James, Charles Lewis, M. M. McCabe, G. E. L. Owen, Malcolm Schofield, David Sedley, Quentin Skinner, Tim Smiley, Richard Tuck, Gregory Vlastos, and Bernard Williams. In opening me to philosophy, they utterly changed my life. In this context I should especially like to thank Bernard Williams, with whom I have been in conversation for over thirty years, for his generosity, his ironic humanity, and simply for being his brilliant self. For me, he is *the* philosopher in our midst.

But, above all, I thank Sophia Lear. Her company, her conversation, her infectious joy are, for me, everywhere evident in this book.

INDEX